Richard Harwood and Ian Lodge

Cambridge IGCSE®

Combined and Co-ordinated Sciences

Chemistry Workbook

CAMBRIDGE UNIVERSITY PRESS

CAMBRIDGE
UNIVERSITY PRESS

University Printing House, Cambridge CB2 8BS, United Kingdom

One Liberty Plaza, 20th Floor, New York, NY 10006, USA

477 Williamstown Road, Port Melbourne, VIC 3207, Australia

4843/24, 2nd Floor, Ansari Road, Daryaganj, Delhi – 110002, India

79 Anson Road, #06–04/06, Singapore 079906

Cambridge University Press is part of the University of Cambridge.

It furthers the University's mission by disseminating knowledge in the pursuit of education, learning and research at the highest international levels of excellence.

www.cambridge.org
Information on this title: www.cambridge.org/9781316631058

First published 2017
20 19 18 17 16 15 14 13 12 11 10 9 8 7 6 5 4

Printed in Malaysia by Vivar Printing

A catalogue record for this publication is available from the British Library

ISBN 978-1-316-63105-8 Paperback

Contents

iii

Introduction

This workbook covers two syllabuses: Cambridge IGCSE Combined Science (0653) and Cambridge IGCSE Co-ordinated Sciences (0654). Before you start using this workbook, check with your teacher which syllabus you are studying and which papers you will take. You will sit either the Core paper or the Extended paper for your syllabus. If you are sitting the Extended paper, you will study the Core material and the Supplement material for your syllabus.

Once you know which paper you will be sitting, you can use the exercises in this workbook to help develop the skills you need and prepare for your examination.

The examination tests three different Assessment Objectives, or AOs for short. These are:

AO1 Knowledge with understanding

AO2 Handling information and problem solving

AO3 Experimental skills and investigations.

In the examination, about 50% of the marks are for AO1, 30% for AO2 and 20% for AO3. Just learning your work and remembering it is therefore not enough to make sure that you get the best possible grade in the exam. Half of all the marks are for AO2 and AO3. You need to be able to use what you've learned in unfamiliar contexts (AO2) and to demonstrate your experimental skills (AO3).

There are lots of activities in your coursebook which will help you to develop your experimental skills by doing practical work. This workbook contains exercises to help you to develop AO2 and AO3 further. There are some questions that just involve remembering things you have been taught (AO1), but most of the questions require you to use what you've learned to work out, for example, what a set of data means, or to suggest how an experiment might be improved.

These exercises are not intended to be exactly like the questions you will get on your exam papers. This is because they are meant to help you to develop your skills, rather than testing you on them.

There's an introduction at the start of each exercise that tells you the purpose of it – which skills you will be working with as you answer the questions.

For some parts of the exercises, there are self-assessment checklists. You can try using these to mark your own work. This will help you to remember the important points to think about. Your teacher should also mark the work and will discuss with you whether your own assessments are right.

There are sidebars in the margins of the book to show which material relates to each syllabus and paper. If there is no sidebar, it means that everyone will study this material.

Use this table to ensure that you study the right material for your syllabus and paper:

Cambridge IGCSE Combined Science (0653)		Cambridge IGCSE Co-ordinated Sciences (0654)	
Core	**Supplement**	**Core**	**Supplement**
You will study the material:	*You will study the material:*	*You will study the material:*	*You will study* **everything**. *This includes the material:*
Without a sidebar	Without a sidebar	Without a sidebar	Without a sidebar
	With a double grey sidebar	With a single grey sidebar	With a single grey sidebar
	With a double black sidebar	With a double grey sidebar	With a double grey sidebar
			With a single black sidebar
			With a double black sidebar

The Periodic Table

Group

Key

	atomic number
	atomic symbol
	name
	relative atomic mass

I	II											III	IV	V	VI	VII	VIII
						1 **H** hydrogen 1											2 **He** helium 4
3 **Li** lithium 7	4 **Be** beryllium 9											5 **B** boron 11	6 **C** carbon 12	7 **N** nitrogen 14	8 **O** oxygen 16	9 **F** fluorine 19	10 **Ne** neon 20
11 **Na** sodium 23	12 **Mg** magnesium 24											13 **Al** aluminium 27	14 **Si** silicon 28	15 **P** phosphorus 31	16 **S** sulfur 32	17 **Cl** chlorine 35.5	18 **Ar** argon 40
19 **K** potassium 39	20 **Ca** calcium 40	21 **Sc** scandium 45	22 **Ti** titanium 48	23 **V** vanadium 51	24 **Cr** chromium 52	25 **Mn** manganese 55	26 **Fe** iron 56	27 **Co** cobalt 59	28 **Ni** nickel 59	29 **Cu** copper 64	30 **Zn** zinc 65	31 **Ga** gallium 70	32 **Ge** germanium 73	33 **As** arsenic 75	34 **Se** selenium 79	35 **Br** bromine 80	36 **Kr** krypton 84
37 **Rb** rubidium 85	38 **Sr** strontium 88	39 **Y** yttrium 89	40 **Zr** zirconium 91	41 **Nb** niobium 93	42 **Mo** molybdenum 96	43 **Tc** technetium –	44 **Ru** ruthenium 101	45 **Rh** rhodium 103	46 **Pd** palladium 106	47 **Ag** silver 108	48 **Cd** cadmium 112	49 **In** indium 115	50 **Sn** tin 119	51 **Sb** antimony 122	52 **Te** tellurium 128	53 **I** iodine 127	54 **Xe** xenon 131
55 **Cs** caesium 133	56 **Ba** barium 137	57–71 lanthanoids	72 **Hf** hafnium 179	73 **Ta** tantalum 181	74 **W** tungsten 184	75 **Re** rhenium 186	76 **Os** osmium 190	77 **Ir** iridium 192	78 **Pt** platinum 195	79 **Au** gold 197	80 **Hg** mercury 201	81 **Tl** thallium 204	82 **Pb** lead 207	83 **Bi** bismuth 209	84 **Po** polonium –	85 **At** astatine –	86 **Rn** radon –
87 **Fr** francium –	88 **Ra** radium –	89–103 actinoids	104 **Rf** rutherfordium –	105 **Db** dubnium –	106 **Sg** seaborgium –	107 **Bh** bohrium –	108 **Hs** hassium –	109 **Mt** meitnerium –	110 **Ds** darmstadtium –	111 **Rg** roentgenium –	112 **Cn** copernicium –		114 **Fl** flerovium –		116 **Lv** livermorium –		

lanthanoids

57 **La** lanthanium 139	58 **Ce** cerium 140	59 **Pr** praseodymium 141	60 **Nd** neodymium 144	61 **Pm** promethium –	62 **Sm** samarium 150	63 **Eu** europium 152	64 **Gd** gadolinium 157	65 **Tb** terbium 159	66 **Dy** dysprosium 163	67 **Ho** holmium 165	68 **Er** erbium 167	69 **Tm** thulium 169	70 **Yb** ytterbium 173	71 **Lu** lutetium 175

actinoids

89 **Ac** actinium –	90 **Th** thorium 232	91 **Pa** protactinium 231	92 **U** uranium 238	93 **Np** neptunium –	94 **Pu** plutonium –	95 **Am** americium –	96 **Cm** curium –	97 **Bk** berkelium –	98 **Cf** californium –	99 **Es** einsteinium –	100 **Fm** fermium –	101 **Md** mendelevium –	102 **No** nobelium –	103 **Lr** lawrencium –

Chapter C1
Planet Earth

Exercise C1.01 Global warming and the 'greenhouse effect'

> This exercise will help in developing your skills at processing unfamiliar data and making deductions from novel sources.

The diagram shows a simplified carbon cycle.

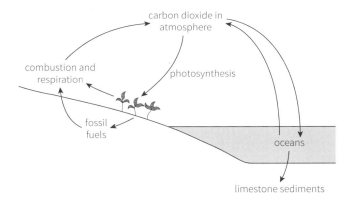

a Describe the process of **photosynthesis** in simple terms.

....

....

....

The '**greenhouse effect**' is caused by heat from the Sun being trapped inside the Earth's atmosphere by some of the gases which are present – their molecules absorb infrared radiation. As the amount of these 'greenhouse gases' increases, the mean (average) temperature of the Earth increases. It is estimated that, if there were no greenhouse effect,' the Earth's temperature would be cooler by 33 °C on average. Some of the gases which cause this effect are carbon dioxide, methane and oxides of nitrogen (NO_x).

Global warming: Since the burning of fossil fuels started to increase in the late nineteenth century, the amount of carbon dioxide in the atmosphere has increased steadily. The changes in the mean temperature of the Earth have not been quite so regular. Below are some data regarding the changes in mean temperature of the Earth and amount of carbon dioxide in the atmosphere. Table 1.01 gives the changes over recent years, while Table 1.02 gives the longer-term changes. The mean temperature is the average over all parts of the Earth's surface over a whole year. The amount of carbon dioxide is given in ppm (parts of carbon dioxide per million parts of air).

Year	CO_2 / ppm	Mean temperature / °C
1982	340	14.08
1984	343	14.15
1986	347	14.19
1988	351	14.41
1990	354	14.48
1992	356	14.15
1994	358	14.31
1996	361	14.36
1998	366	14.70
2000	369	14.39
2002	373	14.67
2004	377	14.58
2006	381	14.63
2008	385	14.51
2010	390	14.69
2012	394	14.59
2014	395	14.70
2016	401	14.83

Table 1.01

Year	CO_2 / ppm	Mean temperature / °C
1880	291	13.92
1890	294	13.81
1900	297	13.95
1910	300	13.80
1920	303	13.82
1930	306	13.96
1940	309	14.14
1950	312	13.83
1960	317	13.99
1970	324	14.04
1980	338	14.28
1990	354	14.48
2000	369	14.39
2010	390	14.69

Table 1.02

b Plot these results on the grid provided using the left-hand *y*-axis for amount of carbon dioxide and the right-hand *y*-axis for mean temperature. Draw **two** separate graphs to enable you to compare the trends. (Use graph paper if you need a larger grid.)

c What do you notice about the trend in amount of carbon dioxide?

....

....

d What do you notice about the trend in mean temperature?

....

....

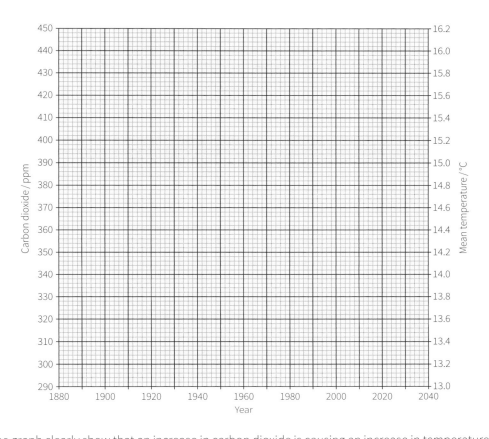

e Does the graph clearly show that an increase in carbon dioxide is causing an increase in temperature?

....

....

f Estimate the amount of carbon dioxide in the atmosphere and the likely mean temperature of the Earth in the years 2020 and 2040.

....

....

g Between the eleventh century and the end of the eighteenth century the amount of carbon dioxide in the atmosphere varied between 275 and 280 ppm. Why did it start to rise from the nineteenth century onwards.

....

h Other 'greenhouse gases' are present in much smaller amounts. However, they are much more effective at keeping in heat than carbon dioxide. Methane (1.7 ppm) has 21 times the effect of carbon dioxide. Nitrogen oxides (0.3 ppm) have 310 times the effect of carbon dioxide.

Name a source that releases each of these gases into the atmosphere.

Methane: ....

Nitrogen oxides: ....

Use the checklist below to give yourself a mark for your graph. For each point, award yourself:

- 2 marks if you did it really well
- 1 mark if you made a good attempt at it, and partly succeeded
- 0 marks if you did not try to do it, or did not succeed.

Self-assessment checklist for graphs:

Check point	Marks awarded	
	You	Your teacher
You have plotted each point precisely and correctly for both sets of data – using the different scales on the two vertical axes.		
You have used a small, neat cross or dot for the points of one graph.		
You have used a small, but different, symbol for the points of the other graph.		
You have drawn the connecting lines through one set of points accurately – using a ruler for the lines.		
You have drawn the connecting lines through the other set of points accurately – using a different colour or broken line.		
You have ignored any anomalous results when drawing the lines.		
Total (out of 12)		

10–12   Excellent.

7–9   Good.

4–6   A good start, but you need to improve quite a bit.

2–3   Poor. Try this same graph again, using a new sheet of graph paper.

1   Very poor. Read through all the criteria again, and then try the same graph again.

Exercise C1.02 Atmospheric pollution, industry and transport

> This exercise discusses different aspects of atmospheric pollution and relates it to key aspects of human activity. It will help you in developing your skills in evaluating data and drawing conclusions from them.

The following pie charts show estimates of the sources of three major atmospheric pollutants in an industrialised country.

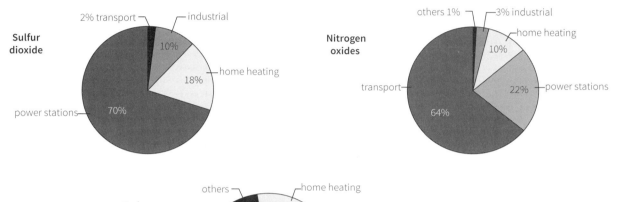

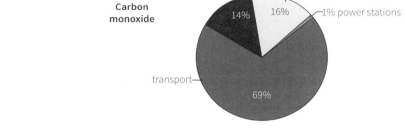

a What is the largest source of sulfur dioxide pollution?

....

b Name the three major fuels whose combustion gives rise to the levels of sulfur dioxide in the atmosphere.

....

c Units are being added to the some power stations and industrial plants to prevent the emission of sulfur dioxide. What is the name given to these units?

....

d Nitrogen oxides (NO_x) are another major pollutant of the atmosphere, particularly in large cities.

    i Nitrogen monoxide is formed by the reaction of nitrogen and oxygen inside the hot engine of cars and other vehicles. Complete the following equation for the reaction producing nitrogen monoxide.

$$N_2 + O_2 \rightarrow ......NO$$

ii When leaving the car, nitrogen monoxide in the exhaust fumes reacts further with oxygen in the air to produce the brown gas which can be seen in the atmosphere over large cities. This gas is nitrogen dioxide. Balance the equation for the production of this gas.

nitrogen monoxide + oxygen $\longrightarrow$ nitrogen dioxide

......NO $\quad + \quad O_2 \quad \rightarrow \quad$ ......NO_2

iii The operating temperature of a diesel engine is significantly higher than that of a petrol (gasoline) engine. Would you expect the level of NO_x emissions from a diesel-powered vehicle to be greater or lower than from a petrol-powered vehicle? Give the reason for your answer.

....

....

iv What attachment is fitted to modern cars to reduce the level of pollution by oxides of nitrogen?

....

e Nitrogen oxides, unburnt hydrocarbons and carbon monoxide combine together under the influence of ultraviolet light to produce photochemical smog.

i Why do you think this form of pollution is most common in large cities?

....

....

ii What other form of pollution from car exhaust fumes has now almost totally disappeared from modern cities following changes in fuel and pollution monitoring?

....

f In order to control traffic flow, London introduced a 'congestion charge' for vehicles entering the centre of the city in 2003. Table 1.03 shows figures for the percentage fall in the levels of certain pollutants following the introduction of the congestion charge.

	Pollutant gas within Congestion Charge Zone	
	NO_x	CO_2
Overall traffic emissions change 2003 versus 2002 / %	−13.4	−16.4
Overall traffic emissions change 2004 versus 2003 / %	−5.2	−0.9
Change due to improved vehicle technology, 2003 to 2006 / %	−17.3	−3.4

Table 1.03

i What was the measured percentage drop in the level of nitrogen oxides within the Congestion Charge Zone over the first 2 years following the introduction of the charge?

....

....

ii At face value there seems to be a drop in the levels of pollutants following the introduction of the congestion charge. But should we expect the fall in pollution levels to continue?

....

iii An independent study published in 2011 suggested that other factors should be taken into account, particularly when trying to study a relatively small area within a large city. One factor is hinted at in the third row of figures. What is that factor; and what other influences need to be taken into account in considering this situation?

....

....

....

....

g The use of fossil fuels in industry and transport also produces carbon dioxide. What is the reasoning behind the slogan painted on these freight containers seen waiting to be loaded on to a freight train outside a major UK station? Outline the argument behind the slogan.

....

....

....

....

....

Exercise C1.03 Clean water is crucial

> This exercise covers aspects of how we produce clean water for domestic and industrial use,
> focusing on stages that depend on key physical and chemical techniques.

The provision of clean drinking water and sanitation to more of the world's population is one of the key millennium goals of the United Nations. The lack of this basic provision impacts not only on the levels of disease in an area, in particular the mortality rate of children, but also on the level of education and the role of women within a community.

The diagram shows the different stages involved in a modern water plant producing water for domestic and industrial use.

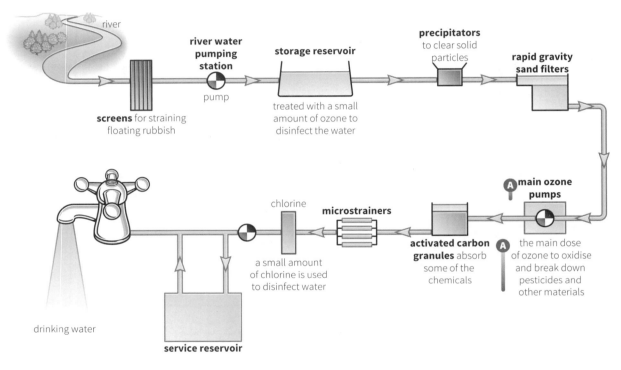

a   What devices are used in the early stages of processing to remove insoluble debris and material?
Include comments on the size of the material removed by these methods.

....

....

....

b   What is the common purpose of treating the water with chlorine and/or ozone?

....

c   What other purpose does treatment with ozone achieve?

....

d What type of chemical agent is ozone (O_3) behaving as in the reactions involved in part **c**?

....

e Countries that have insufficient rainfall, or where water supply is in great demand, may need to use other methods of producing clean water. Here, processes for **desalination** are used.

i What does the term 'desalination' mean?

....

ii Name **two** methods that such countries use for desalination.

....

iii Give one disadvantage of these methods of desalination.

....

f Tap water produced by a water treatment plant such as shown in the diagram is clean, but it is not pure. It will contain metal and non-metal ions dissolved from the rocks that the rivers and streams have flowed over.

i Chloride ions are present in tap water. Describe a chemical test that would show the presence of chloride ions (Cl^-) in the water. Describe the test and what would be observed.

....

....

....

ii One of the chlorides often present in tap water is sodium chloride. Give the word and balanced symbol equation for the reaction taking place in the test you have described above.

sodium chloride   + ... $\rightarrow$ ....   + ...

NaCl   + ... $\rightarrow$ ....   + ...

iii Give the ionic equation for the reaction taking place (include state symbols).

....

🔑 **KEY TERMS**

physical state: the three states of matter are solid, liquid and gas

condensation: the change of state from gas to liquid

melting: the change of state from solid to liquid

freezing: the change of state from liquid to solid at the melting point

boiling: the change of state from liquid to gas at the boiling point of the liquid

evaporation: the change of state from liquid to gas below the boiling point

sublimation: the change of state directly from solid to gas (or the reverse)

crystallisation: the formation of crystals when a saturated solution is left to cool

filtration: the separation of a solid from a liquid using filter paper

distillation: the separation of a liquid from a mixture using differences in boiling point

fractional distillation: the separation of a mixture of liquids using differences in boiling point

diffusion: the random movement of particles in a fluid (liquid or gas) leading to the complete mixing of the particles

chromatography: the separation of a mixture of soluble (coloured) substances using paper and a solvent

atom: the smallest part of an element that can take part in a chemical change

proton number (atomic number): the number of protons in the nucleus of an atom of an element

nucleon number (mass number): the number of protons and neutrons in the nucleus of an atom

electron arrangement: the organisation of electrons in their different energy levels (shells)

isotopes: atoms of the same element which have the same proton number but a different nucleon number

Exercise C2.01 Changing physical state

This exercise will develop your understanding of the kinetic model and the energy changes involved in changes of physical state.

The graph shows the heating curve for a pure substance. The temperature rises with time as the substance is heated.

a What physical state(s) is the substance in at points **A**, **B**, **C** and **D**?

A .... B ....

C .... D ....

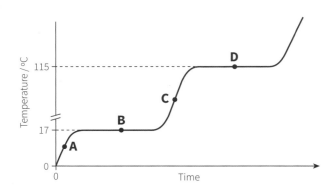

b What is the melting point of the substance? ....

c What is its boiling point? ....

d What happens to the temperature while the substance is changing state?

....

e The substance is not water. How do we know this from the graph?

....

f Complete the passage using the words given below.

different	diffusion	gas	spread	particles
diffuse	random	lattice	vibrate	temperature

The kinetic model states that the .... in a liquid and a .... are in constant motion.

In a gas, the particles are far apart from each other and their motion is said to be .... The particles in a

solid are held in fixed positions in a regular .... In a solid, the particles can only .... about

their fixed positions.

Liquids and gases are fluid states. When particles move in a fluid, they can collide with each other.

When they collide, they bounce off each other in .... directions. If two gases or liquids are mixed,

the different types of particle .... out and get mixed up. This process is called ....

At the same .... particles that have a lower mass move faster than those with higher mass.

This means that the lighter particles will spread and mix more quickly; the lighter particles are said to

.... faster than the heavier particles.

g Use the data given for the substances listed in Table 2.01 to answer the questions that follow on their physical state at a room temperature of 25 °C and atmospheric pressure.

Substance	Melting point / °C	Boiling point / °C
sodium	98	883
radon	−71	−62
ethanol	−117	78
cobalt	1492	2900
nitrogen	−210	−196
propane	−188	−42
ethanoic acid	16	118

Table 2.01

i   Which substance is a liquid over the smallest range of temperature? ....

ii   Which **two** substances are gaseous at −50 °C? .... and ....

iii Which substance has the lowest freezing point? ....

iv   Which substance is liquid at 2500 °C? ....

v   A sample of ethanoic acid was found to boil at 121 °C at atmospheric pressure. Use the information in the table to comment on this result.

....

....

Exercise C2.02 Plotting a cooling curve

This exercise presents data obtained practically for plotting a cooling curve. It will help develop your skills in handling the data and interpreting what changes the different regions of the curve represent. Examples of sublimation are also discussed.

A student carried out the following data-logging experiment using apparatus shown in the following diagram as part of a project on changes of state. An organic crystalline solid was melted by placing it in a tube in a boiling water bath. A temperature sensor was placed in the liquid.

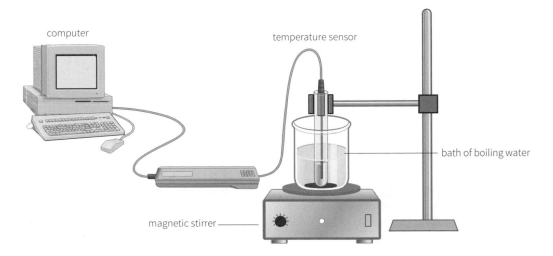

The temperature change was followed as the liquid was allowed to cool down. The data shown in Table 2.02 are taken from the computer record of the temperature change as the liquid cooled down to room temperature.

Time / min	0	0.5	1.0	1.5	2.0	2.2	2.4	2.6	2.8	3.0	3.5	4.0	4.5	5.0
Temperature / °C	96.1	89.2	85.2	82.0	80.9	80.7	80.6	80.6	80.5	80.3	78.4	74.2	64.6	47.0

Table 2.02

a   On the grid provided, plot a graph of the temperature change taking place in this experiment.

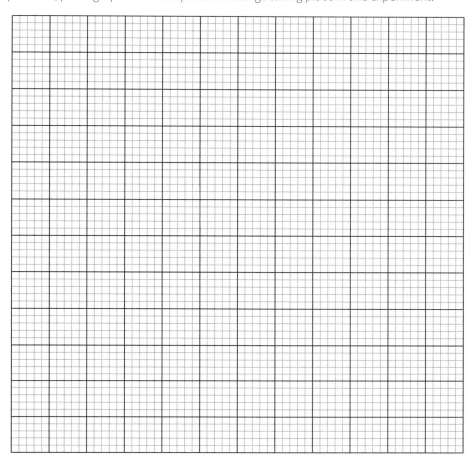

b   What change is taking place over the second minute of the experiment?

....

c   Why does the temperature remain almost constant over this period of time? Give your explanation in terms of what is happening to the organisation of the molecules of the substance.

....

....

....

....

d   What change would need to be made to carry out the experiment using a compound with a melting point greater than 100 °C?

....

e A similar experiment was carried out to demonstrate the cooling curve for paraffin wax.

    i In the space below, sketch the shape of the graph you would expect to produce.

    ii Explain why the curve is the shape you have drawn.

    ....

    ....

f Sublimation occurs when a substance passes between the solid and gaseous states without going through the liquid phase. Both carbon dioxide and water can sublime under certain conditions of temperature and pressure.

'Dry ice' is the solid form of carbon dioxide used in commercial refrigeration. At atmospheric pressure it has a 'sublimation point' of −78.5 °C.

    i What difference can you see between solid carbon dioxide and water ice at atmospheric pressure?

    ....

    ....

    ii If you gently shake a carbon dioxide fire extinguisher as seen in the diagram, you will feel the presence of liquid within the extinguisher. What conditions within the extinguisher mean that the CO_2 is liquid in this case?

    ....

    ....

    iii Complete the following paragraph about a particular type of frost using the words listed below.

surrounding	**liquid**	**colder**	**humid**
white	**crystals**	**ice**	

Hoar frost is a powdery .... frost caused when solid .... forms from .... air. The solid surface on which it is formed must be .... than the .... air.

Water vapour is deposited on a surface as fine ice .... without going through the .... phase.

Exercise C2.03 Diffusion, solubility and separation

> The processes of diffusion and dissolving in a solvent are linked. This exercise explores the basis of these processes in terms of the kinetic (particle) theory. The separation of a solvent mixture by fractional distillation is discussed.

A student placed some crystals of potassium manganate(VII) at the bottom of a beaker of distilled water. She then left the contents of the beaker to stand for 1 h.

a The diagram below shows what she saw during the experiment.

After 1 h, all the solid crystals had disappeared and the solution was purple throughout.

distilled water

purple crystals

at start   after 15 min   after 1 h

i Use the ideas of the kinetic theory to explain her observations.

....

....

....

....

ii If warm water at 50 °C had been used, would the observations have taken place in a longer or shorter time? Explain your answer.

....

....

....

b The process of dissolving can be used to separate and purify chemical compounds. Organic solvents such as propanone can be used to extract pigments from plants. Some grass is crushed and mixed with the propanone. The colour pigments are extracted to give a dark green solution.

i Given a pure sample of chlorophyll, describe how could you show that the green solution from the grass contained chlorophyll and other coloured pigments?

....

....

....

....

15

ii Draw a labelled diagram that describes the method of separating coloured pigments that you have discussed in part **i**.

Use the checklist below to give yourself a mark for your drawing. For each point, award yourself:
- **2 marks if you did it really well**
- **1 mark if you made a good attempt at it, and partly succeeded**
- **0 marks if you did not try to do it, or did not succeed.**

Self-assessment checklist for drawings:

Check point	Marks awarded	
	You	Your teacher
You have made a large drawing, using the space provided.		
There are no obvious errors – liquids missing, flasks open when they should be closed, etc.		
You have drawn single lines with a sharp pencil, not many tries at the same line (and erased mistakes).		
You have used a ruler for the lines that are straight.		
Your diagram is in the right proportions.		
You have drawn label lines with a ruler, touching the item being labelled.		
You have written the labels horizontally and neatly, well away from the diagram itself.		
Total (out of 14)		

12–14   Excellent.

10–11   Good.

7–9   A good start, but you need to improve quite a bit.

5–6   Poor. Try this same drawing again, using a new sheet of paper.

1–4   Very poor. Read through all the criteria again, and then try the same drawing.

   iii   Explain the role of chlorophyll in the leaves of green plants.

....

....

....

....

c   Propanone is a very useful solvent that mixes well with water even though it is an organic compound.
A propanone : water (65% : 35%) mixture used for cleaning laboratory apparatus can be separated using
fractional distillation.

A total volume of 80 cm³ of the mixture was distilled.

Sketch below a graph of the temperature readings against the volume of distillate collected for the
distillation carried out. The thermometer is placed at the connection between the fractionating column and
the condenser. The boiling point of propanone is 56 °C.

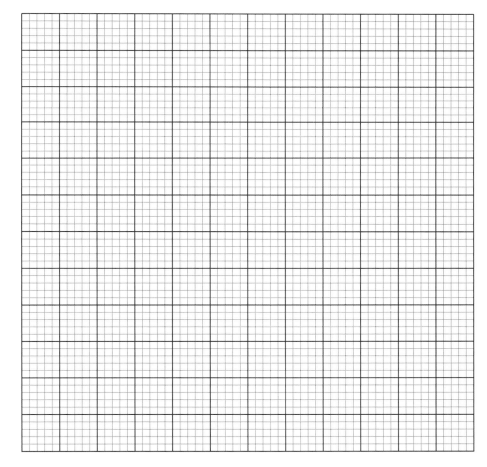

Exercise C2.04 Chromatography at the races

> This exercise will help you understand aspects of chromatography by considering an unfamiliar application of the technique.

Chromatography is used by the 'Horse Racing Forensic Laboratory' to test for the presence of illegal drugs in racehorses.

A concentrated sample of urine is spotted on to chromatography paper on the start line. Alongside this, known drugs are spotted. The chromatogram is run using methanol as the solvent. When finished, the paper is read by placing it under ultraviolet light. A chromatogram of urine from four racehorses is shown in the following diagram and details are included in Table 2.03.

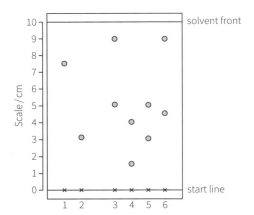

Spot	Description
1	caffeine
2	paracetamol
3	urine sample horse **A**
4	urine sample horse **B**
5	urine sample horse **C**
6	urine sample horse **D**

Table 2.03

a State two factors which determine the distance a substance travels up the paper.

....

....

b The results show that the sample from one horse contains an illegal substance. State which horse and the drug that is present.

....

c Give a reason for the use of this drug.

....

d The results for known drugs are given as 'R_f values'.

$$R_f = \frac{\text{distance travelled by the substance}}{\text{distance travelled by the solvent}}$$

Calculate the R_f value for caffeine.

Exercise C2.05 Atomic structure

> This exercise helps familiarise you with aspects of atomic structure including the organisation of electrons into energy levels (or shells), and the uses of radioactivity.

a Choose from the words below to fill in the gaps in the passage. Words may be used once, more than once or not at all.

proton	electrons	nucleon	isotopes
neutrons	nucleus	energy levels	protons

Atoms are made up of three different particles: .... which are positively charged; ....

which have no charge; and .... which are negatively charged. The negatively charged particles

are arranged in different .... (shells) around the .... of the atom. The particles with

a negligible mass are the .... All atoms of the same element contain the same number

of .... and .... Atoms of the same element with different numbers of .... are

known as ....

b This part of the exercise is concerned with electron arrangements and the structure of the Periodic Table. Complete these sentences by filling in the blanks with words or numbers.

The electrons in an atom are arranged in a series of .... around the nucleus. These shells are also

called .... levels. In an atom, the shell .... to the nucleus fills first, then the next shell,

and so on. There is room for:

- up to .... electrons in the first shell
- up to .... electrons in the second shell
- up to .... electrons in the third shell.

(There are 18 electrons in total when the three shells are completely full.)

The elements in the Periodic Table are organised in the same way as the electrons fill the shells. Shells fill

from .... to .... across the .... of the Periodic Table.

- The first shell fills up first from .... to helium.
- The second shell fills next from lithium to ....
- Eight .... go into the third shell from sodium to argon.
- Then the fourth shell starts to fill from potassium.

c In 1986, an explosion at Chernobyl in the Ukraine released a radioactive cloud containing various radioactive isotopes. Three such isotopes are mentioned in Table 2.04. Use your Periodic Table to answer the following questions about them.

Element	Nucleon (mass) number
strontium	90
iodine	131
caesium	137

Table 2.04

i How many electrons are there in one atom of strontium-90? ....

ii How many protons are there in one atom of iodine-131? ....

iii How many neutrons are there in an atom of caesium-137? ....

Exercise C2.06 Influential organisation

This exercise explores how that structure influences the major properties of the atoms of an element.

The way in which the subatomic particles are organised within an atom gives rise to the characteristic properties of that atom. Whether an atom is radioactive, the type of bond it makes, its chemical reactivity and its position in the Periodic Table are all dependent on this organisation.

a Isotopes of certain elements, such as carbon-14, can be of use in biochemical and medical research. Because they are radioactive, they can be used by scientists to track the synthesis and use of compounds important in the chemistry of cells and tissues.

i Complete Table 2.05 about the isotopes of some common elements, making deductions from the information given. For each element, the second isotope is a radioisotope used in research.

Isotope	Name of element	Proton number	Nucleon number	Number of		
				p	n	e
$^{12}_{6}C$	carbon	6	12	6	6	6
$^{14}_{6}C$						
$^{1}_{1}H$			1			
$^{3}_{1}H$	hydrogen (tritium)					
$^{31}_{15}P$		15	31			
$^{32}_{15}P$						
$^{127}_{53}I$	iodine			53		53
$^{131}_{53}I$				53		

Table 2.05

ii Researchers are able to use these radioisotopes to study the chemistry of cells because these atoms have the same chemical properties as the non-radioactive atoms. Why are the chemical properties of all isotopes of the same element identical?

....

....

....

b The table below gives details of the atomic structure of five atoms, **A**, **B**, **C**, **D** and **E**. (Note that these letters are **not** their chemical symbols.)

Complete Table 2.06 to show the electron arrangement of each of the atoms.

Atom	Proton number	Electron arrangement			
		1st shell	**2nd shell**	**3rd shell**	**4th shell**
A	2				
B	5				
C	13				
D	15				
E	19				

Table 2.06

i How many of these atoms are of elements in the second period of the Periodic Table?

....

ii Which two atoms belong to elements in the same group?

....

iii How many electrons does atom **C** have which would be involved in chemical bonding?

....

iv Draw a diagram to show the arrangement of the electrons in atom **D**.

Chapter C3
Elements and compounds

KEY TERMS

element: a substance containing only one type of atom

compound: a substance made of two, or more, elements chemically combined together

periodic table: the table in which the elements are organised in order of increasing proton number and electron arrangement

group: a vertical column of elements in the Periodic Table; elements in the same group have similar properties

period: a horizontal row of elements in the Periodic Table

valency: the number of chemical bonds an atom can make

Exercise C3.01   Periodic patterns in the properties of the elements

This exercise will help your understanding of the periodic, or repeating, patterns shown by the elements. It will also support your understanding of the structure of the Periodic Table in groups of elements and help you begin to predict properties within these groups.

One physical property that shows a periodic change linked to the Periodic Table is the melting point of an element. Below is a chart of the melting points of the elements in Periods 2 and 3 plotted against the proton number of the element.

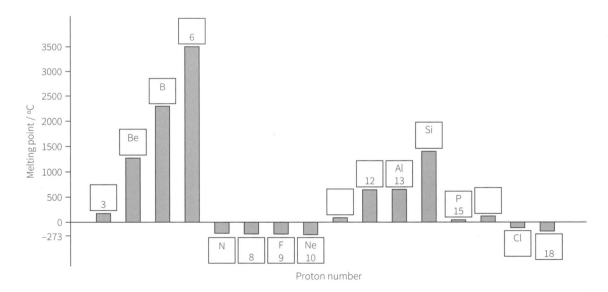

a Fill in the symbols and proton numbers missing from the boxes on the chart above (seven symbols and seven proton numbers).

b Which **two** elements are at the peaks of the chart?

.... and ....

c To which group do these two elements belong? ....

d The halogens are one group of elements in the Periodic Table. Complete the following statements about the halogens by crossing out the incorrect bold words.

• The halogens are **metals / non-metals** and their vapours are **coloured / colourless**.

• The halogens are **toxic / non-toxic** to humans.

• Halogen molecules are each made of **one / two** atoms; they are **monatomic / diatomic**.

• Halogens react with **metal / non-metal** elements to form crystalline compounds that are salts.

• The halogens get **more / less** reactive going down the group in the Periodic Table.

• Halogens can **colour / bleach** vegetable dyes and kill bacteria.

e Elements within a group tend to show clear trends in their physical properties as you go down a group. The following solid elements in Group VI show this. Complete Table 3.01 by filling in the gaps. Use the following values when filling in the missing values.

685   4.79   0.198   450   0.221

Name of element	sulfur	selenium	tellurium
density / g/cm³	2.07		6.24
melting point / °C	115	221	
boiling point / °C	445		988
ionic radius / nm	0.184		

Table 3.01

Exercise C3.02 The first four periods

> This exercise is aimed at developing your knowledge of the basic features of the Periodic Table and the properties of an element that relate to its position in the table.

The diagram below shows the upper part of the Periodic Table with certain elements selected.

Using the elements shown above, write down the symbols for the elements which answer the following questions.

a Which **two** elements are stored under oil because they are very reactive?

....

b Which **two** elements are transition metals?

....

c Which element has just two electrons in the full outer shell of its atom?

....

d Which element is a red-brown liquid at room temperature and pressure?

....

e Which element has four electrons in the outer energy level of its atom?

....

f Which element is a yellow solid at room temperature?

....

g Which elements are noble gases?

....

h Which element has compounds that produce blue solutions when they dissolve?

....

i Which element has the electron arrangement 2.8.8.2?

....

j Which element burns with a brilliant white flame when ignited?

....

Exercise C3.03 Trends in the halogens

This exercise examines the trends in physical properties of elements within a non-metal group of the Periodic Table. It should help you develop your skills at analysing and predicting trends within a group.

Table 3.02 shows some of the physical properties of the elements of Group VII at atmospheric pressure. These elements are known as the halogens and the properties show distinct trends as you go down the group.

Element	Proton number	Melting point / °C	Boiling point / °C	Colour
fluorine	9	−219	−188	pale yellow
chlorine	17	−101	−34	pale green
bromine	35	−6		
iodine	53	114	185	grey-black
astatine	85	303	337	

Table 3.02

a   Plot a graph of the melting points and boiling points of the halogens against their proton numbers in the grid provided. Join the points for each property together to produce two separate lines on the graph.

Draw a line across the graph at 20 °C (room temperature) to help you decide which elements are solid, liquid or gas at room temperature and pressure.

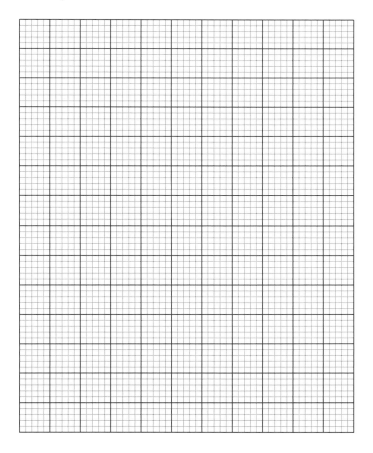

b Use your graph to estimate the boiling point of bromine, and state its colour and physical state at room temperature.

Estimated boiling point: .... °C   Colour: ....

Physical state: ....

c Which of the halogens are gases at room temperature and pressure?

....

d Astatine is very rarely seen. What would you predict to be its physical state and colour at room temperature and pressure?

....

e What is the trend observed in the melting points of the halogens as you go down the group?

....

Exercise C3.04 The chemical bonding in simple molecules

This exercise will familiarise you with the structures of some simple covalent compounds and the methods we have for representing the structure and shape of their molecules.

a Many covalent compounds exist as simple molecules where the atoms are joined together with single or double bonds. A covalent bond, made up of a shared pair of electrons, is often represented by a short straight line. Complete Table 3.03 by filling in the blank spaces.

Name of compound	Formula	Drawing of structure	Molecular model
hydrogen chloride		H — Cl	
water	H_2O		
ammonia			
	CH_4		
ethene			
		O=C=O	

Table 3.03

b Silicon(IV) oxide is a very common compound in the crust of the Earth. It has a giant covalent structure similar to diamond. Summarise the features of the structure of silicon(IV) oxide (silica), as shown in the diagram, by completing the following statements.

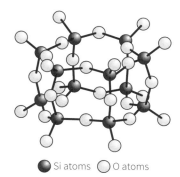

● Si atoms ◯ O atoms

• The strong bonds between the atoms are .... bonds.

• In the crystal, there are two oxygen atoms for every silicon atom, so the formula is ....

• The atoms of the lattice are organised in a .... arrangement like diamond, with a silicon atom at the centre of each ....

• This is an example of a .... structure.

• Each oxygen atom forms .... covalent bonds.

• Each silicon atom forms .... covalent bonds.

c Graphite is one of the crystalline forms of carbon. Two of the distinctive properties of graphite are:

• it conducts electricity even though it is a non-metal, and
• it can act as a lubricant even though it has a giant covalent structure.

Give a brief explanation of these properties in the light of the structure of graphite.

i Graphite as an electrical conductor

....

....

....

ii Graphite as a lubricant

....

....

....

Exercise C3.05 Formulae of ionic compounds

The writing of chemical formulae is central to chemistry. This exercise will help you understand how to work out the formulae of ionic compounds and what such formulae mean.

Table 3.04 shows the valencies and formulae of some common ions.

		Valency		
		1	2	3
Positive ions (cations)	metals	sodium (Na^+) potassium (K^+) silver (Ag^+)	magnesium (Mg^{2+}) copper (Cu^{2+}) zinc (Zn^{2+}) iron (Fe^{2+})	aluminium (Al^{3+}) iron (Fe^{3+}) chromium (Cr^{3+})
	compound ions	ammonium (NH_4^+)		
Negative ions (anions)	non-metals	chloride (Cl^-) bromide (Br^-) iodide (I^-)	oxide (O^{2-}) sulfide (S^{2-})	nitride (N^{3-})
	compound ions	nitrate (NO_3^-) hydroxide (OH^-)	carbonate (CO_3^{2-}) sulfate (SO_4^{2-})	phosphate (PO_4^{3-})

Table 3.04

a   Use the information in the table to work out the formulae of the following ionic compounds.

   i   Copper oxide   ....

   ii   Sodium carbonate   ....

   iii   Zinc sulfate   ....

   iv   Silver nitrate   ....

   v   Magnesium bromide   ....

   vi   Ammonium sulfate   ....

   vii   Magnesium nitride   ....

   viii   Potassium phosphate   ....

   ix   Iron(ɪɪɪ) hydroxide   ....

   x   Chromium(ɪɪɪ) chloride   ....

b   Use the information in the table and your answers in **a** above to give the ratio of the different atoms in the following compounds.

   i   Copper oxide   Cu:O   ....

   ii   Magnesium bromide   Mg:Br   ....

   iii   Magnesium nitride   Mg:N   ....

   iv   Iron(ɪɪɪ) hydroxide   Fe:O:H   ....

   v   Ammonium sulfate   N:H:S:O   ....

c The diagram below shows a representation of the structure of an ionic oxide.

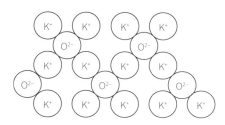

i What is the ratio of K^+ ions to O^{2-} ions? ....

ii What is the formula of this compound? ....

d The following diagram shows the structure of common salt.

i Extend the structure to the right, by adding **four** more ions.

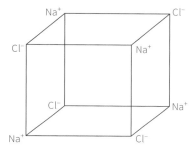

ii Complete the diagrams below for the ions in the structure to show their electron arrangement. Draw in any missing electron shells, showing clearly the origin of the electrons involved.

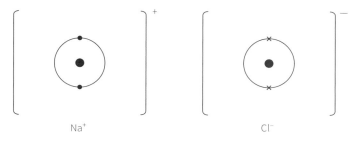

iii Draw an ionic diagram similar to the one above for the structure of magnesium chloride.

Exercise C3.06 The bonding in covalent molecules

> The representation of the structures of covalent molecules is another important feature of chemistry. This exercise helps you develop your understanding of such structures and how to draw dot-and-cross diagrams of the sharing of electrons in these compounds.

Complete Table 3.05 with dot-and-cross and structural diagrams to represent the bonding in the following simple molecular compounds. In the dot-and-cross diagrams, show only the outer shells of the atoms involved.

Molecule	Dot-and-cross diagram	Structure
Ammonia (NH_3)		
Water (H_2O)		
Hydrogen chloride (HCl)		
Ethane (C_2H_6)		
Ethene (C_2H_4)		
Ethanol (C_2H_5OH)		

Table 3.05

Exercise C3.07 The nature of ionic lattices

This exercise will help you relate the structures of ionic compounds to some of their key properties.

The diagram shows a model of the structure of sodium chloride and similar ionic crystals. The ions are arranged in a regular lattice structure – a giant ionic lattice.

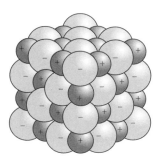

The boxes below contain properties of ionic compounds and their explanations. Draw lines to link each pair.

Property

The solution of an ionic compound in water is a good conductor of electricity – such ionic substances are electrolytes.

Ionic crystals have a regular shape. All the crystals of each solid ionic compound are the same shape. Whatever the size of the crystal, the angles between the faces of the crystal are always the same.

Ionic compounds have relatively high melting points.

When an ionic compound is heated above its melting point, the molten compound is a good conductor of electricity.

Explanation

The ions in the giant ionic structure are always arranged in the same regular way – see the diagram.

The giant ionic structure is held together by the strong attraction between the positive and negative ions. It takes a lot of energy to break down the regular arrangement of ions.

In a molten ionic compound, the positive and negative ions can move around – they can move to the electrodes when a voltage is applied.

In a solution of an ionic compound, the positive metal ions and the negative non-metal ions can move around – they can move to the electrodes when a voltage is applied.

Exercise C3.08 Giant molecular lattices

There are covalent substances where the bonding extends throughout the crystal.
This exercise considers three major macromolecular structures and how their properties
relate to their structure.

Sand is a powder of silicon(IV) oxide (sometimes called silica or silicon dioxide). Its structure is shown
in the diagram.

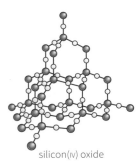

silicon(IV) oxide

a Complete the following statements about the structure of silicon(IV) oxide by crossing out the incorrect
bold words.

Silicon(IV) oxide occurs naturally as **mud / sand**. It has a giant **covalent / electrostatic** structure very similar to
graphite / diamond. Such a structure can also be described as a **micromolecule / macromolecule** as all the
atoms in the crystal are joined together by covalent bonds.

Each silicon atom is bonded to **four / two** oxygen atoms, while each oxygen atom is linked covalently to **four /
two** silicon atoms. The oxygen atoms are arranged **hexagonally / tetrahedrally** around the silicon atoms.

The fact that all the atoms are bonded together in a **two-dimensional / three-dimensional** structure like
graphite / diamond means that silicon(IV) oxide has similar physical properties to **graphite / diamond**. Silica is
very hard / slippery and has a **low / high** melting point. All the outer electrons of the atoms in the structure
are used in making the covalent bonds between the atoms. This means that silicon(IV) oxide **does / does not**
conduct electricity. There are no electrons free to carry the current through the crystal.

b Table 3.06 shows observations and explanations for diamond, graphite and silica. Complete the table by
filling in the gaps. The first section has been completed for you; other sections are only partly complete.

Observation	Explanation
Diamond and silica are both very hard substances …	… because all the atoms in the structure are joined by strong covalent bonds
Diamond does not conduct electricity …	… because
Graphite is …	… because the layers in the structure are only held together by weak forces
	… because there are some free electrons that are able to move between the layers to carry the current

Table 3.06

32

Exercise C3.09 Making magnesium oxide – a quantitative investigation

This exercise will develop your skills in processing and interpreting results from practical work.

Magnesium oxide is made when magnesium is burnt in air. How does the mass of magnesium oxide made depend on the mass of magnesium burnt? The practical method is described below.

Method

- Weigh an empty crucible and lid.

- Roll some magnesium ribbon round a pencil, then remove the coiled ribbon and place it in the crucible and re-weigh (not forgetting the lid).

- Place the crucible in a pipeclay triangle sitting safely on a tripod. (The lid should be on the crucible as shown in the diagram.)

- Heat the crucible and contents strongly, occasionally lifting the lid to allow more air in.

- When the reaction has eased, take off the lid.

- Heat strongly for another 3 min.

- Let the crucible cool down and then weigh it.

- Repeat the heating until the mass is constant.

33

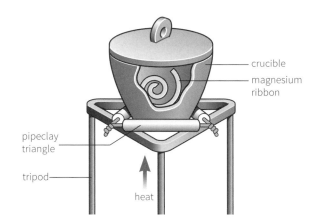

Results

Table 3.07 shows a set of class results calculated from the weights each student group obtained using this method.

Mass of magnesium / g	0.06	0.05	0.04	0.18	0.16	0.10	0.11	0.14	0.15	0.14	0.08	0.10	0.13
Mass of magnesium oxide / g	0.10	0.08	0.06	0.28	0.25	0.15	0.15	0.21	0.24	0.23	0.13	0.17	0.21

Table 3.07

Use these results to plot a graph on the grid provided relating mass of magnesium oxide made to mass of magnesium used. Remember there is one point on this graph that you can be certain of – what point is that? Include it on your graph.

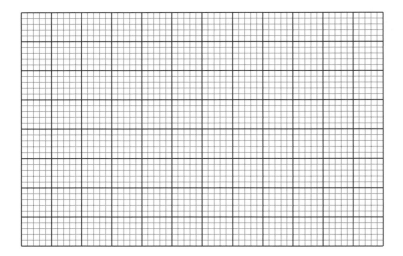

Use the checklist below to give yourself a mark for your graph. For each point, award yourself:

- **2 marks if you did it really well**
- **1 mark if you made a good attempt at it, and partly succeeded**
- **0 marks if you did not try to do it, or did not succeed.**

Self-assessment checklist for graphs:

Check point	Marks awarded	
	You	Your teacher
You have drawn the axes with a ruler, using most of the width and height of the grid.		
You have used a good scale for the x-axis and the y-axis, going up in 0.01 s, 0.05 s or 0.10 s.		
You have labelled the axes correctly, giving the correct units for the scales on both axes.		
You have plotted each point precisely and correctly.		
You have used a small, neat cross for each point.		
You have drawn a single, clear best-fit line through the points – using a ruler for a straight line.		
You have ignored any anomalous results when drawing the line.		
Total (out of 14)		

12–14 Excellent.

10–11 Good.

7–9 A good start, but you need to improve quite a bit.

5–6 Poor. Try this same graph again, using a new sheet of graph paper.

1–4 Very poor. Read through all the criteria again, and then try the same graph again.

a How does the mass of magnesium oxide depend on the starting mass of magnesium?

....

b Work out from the graph the mass of magnesium oxide that you would get from 0.12 g of magnesium

(show the lines you use for this on your graph) .... g

c What mass of oxygen combines with 0.12 g of magnesium? .... g

d What mass of oxygen combines with 24 g of magnesium? .... g

e What is the formula of magnesium oxide, worked out on the basis of these results?
(Relative atomic masses: Mg = 24, O = 16.)

....

....

KEY TERMS

synthesis: the formation of a more complex compound from its elements (or simple substances)

decomposition: the breakdown of a compound into simpler substances

precipitation: the sudden formation of a solid during a chemical reaction

oxidation: the addition of oxygen to an element or compound

reduction: the removal of oxygen from a compound

electrolysis: the decomposition (breakdown) of an ionic compound by the passage of an electric current

electrolyte: a compound which conducts electricity when molten or in solution in water and is decomposed in the process

combustion: the burning of an element or compound in air or oxygen

displacement: a reaction in which a more reactive element displaces a less reactive element from a solution of a salt

USEFUL REACTIONS AND THEIR EQUATIONS

copper carbonate $\longrightarrow$ copper oxide + carbon dioxide

$\quad$ $CuCO_3(s)$ $\quad$ $\longrightarrow$ $\quad$ $CuO(s)$ $\quad$ + $\quad$ $CO_2(g)$ $\qquad\qquad$ thermal decomposition

magnesium + oxygen $\longrightarrow$ magnesium oxide

$\quad$ $2Mg(s)$ $\quad$ + $O_2(g)$ $\longrightarrow$ $\quad$ $2MgO(s)$ $\qquad\qquad$ synthesis (oxidation)

copper oxide + hydrogen $\longrightarrow$ copper + water

$\quad$ $CuO(s)$ $\quad$ + $\quad$ $H_2(g)$ $\quad$ $\longrightarrow$ $Cu(s)$ + $H_2O(l)$ $\qquad\qquad$ reduction

methane + oxygen $\longrightarrow$ carbon dioxide + water

$\quad$ $CH_4(g)$ + $O_2(g)$ $\longrightarrow$ $\quad$ $CO_2(g)$ $\quad$ + $2H_2O(l)$ $\qquad\qquad$ combustion

potassium iodide + chlorine $\longrightarrow$ potassium chloride + iodine

$\quad$ $2KI(aq)$ $\quad$ + $Cl_2(g)$ $\longrightarrow$ $\quad$ $2KCl(aq)$ $\quad$ + $I_2(aq)$ $\qquad\qquad$ displacement

copper(II) sulfate + zinc $\longrightarrow$ zinc sulfate + copper

$\quad$ $CuSO_4(aq)$ $\quad$ + $Zn(s)$ $\longrightarrow$ $ZnSO_4(aq)$ + $Cu(s)$ $\qquad\qquad$ displacement

Exercise C4.01 Key chemical reactions

This exercise is designed to support your understanding of the basic aspects of some important types of chemical reaction.

a Complete the diagrams to show what substances are used and what is produced in burning, respiration and rusting.

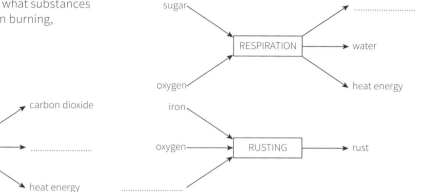

sugar ....

RESPIRATION → water

oxygen → heat energy

hydrocarbon fuel → carbon dioxide

BURNING → ....

oxygen → heat energy

iron

oxygen → RUSTING → rust

....

b What type of chemical change is involved in all of the above reactions? ....

c Oxidation and reduction reactions are important. There are several definitions of oxidation and reduction. Complete the following statements.

- If a substance **gains** oxygen during a reaction, it is ....

- If a substance .... oxygen during a reaction, it is **reduced**.

d The diagram shows **A** the oxidation of copper to copper(II) oxide and **B** the reduction of copper oxide back to copper using hydrogen.

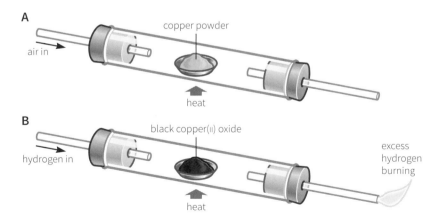

A

copper powder

air in

heat

B

black copper(II) oxide

hydrogen in

excess hydrogen burning

heat

i Fill in the boxes on the equation shown in the diagram with the appropriate terms.

ii What type of agent is hydrogen acting as in this reaction? ....

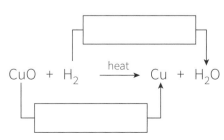

$$CuO + H_2 \xrightarrow{\text{heat}} Cu + H_2O$$

e A further definition links oxidation and reduction to the exchange of electrons during a reaction.

    i Complete the following statements.

        • Oxidation is the .... of electrons.

        • Reduction is the .... of electrons.

    ii Fill in the boxes on the ionic equation shown in the diagram below with the appropriate terms.

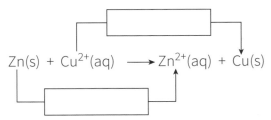

$$Zn(s) + Cu^{2+}(aq) \longrightarrow Zn^{2+}(aq) + Cu(s)$$

    iii What type of agent are copper(II) ions acting as in this reaction? ....

Exercise C4.02 The action of heat on metal carbonates

> **This exercise will help you recall one of the major types of chemical reaction and help develop your skill at deducing conclusions from practical work.**

The carbonates of many metallic elements decompose when heated.

a What type of reaction is this?

....

b Name the gas produced during the breakdown of a metal carbonate, and describe a chemical test for this gas.

....

....

c A student investigates the breakdown of five different metal carbonates using the apparatus shown in the following diagram.

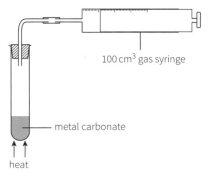

100 cm³ gas syringe

metal carbonate

heat

She heats a 0.010 mol sample of each carbonate using the blue flame of the same Bunsen burner. She measures the time it takes for 100 cm³ of gas to be collected in the gas syringe. Table 4.01 shows her results.

Carbonate	Time taken to collect 100 cm³ of gas / s
metal **A** carbonate	20
metal **B** carbonate	105
metal **C** carbonate	320
metal **D** carbonate	no gas produced after 1000
metal **E** carbonate	60

Table 4.01

In fact, the student used samples of calcium carbonate, copper(II) carbonate, magnesium carbonate, sodium carbonate and zinc carbonate.

Given the information that the more reactive a metal is, the less easy it is to break down the metal carbonate, complete Table 4.02 to show the identity of each metal **A**, **B**, **C**, **D** and **E**.

Metal	Name of metal
A	
B	
C	
D	
E	

Table 4.02

d Write the chemical equation for the breakdown of zinc carbonate.

....

Exercise C4.03 The nature of electrolysis

> This exercise will help you summarise the major aspects of electrolysis and its applications.

a Complete the following passage by using the words listed below.

anode	electrodes	current	molten	electrolyte	solution
positive	hydrogen	molecules	lose	oxygen	cathode

Changes taking place during electrolysis

During electrolysis ionic compounds are decomposed by the passage of an electric current. For this to happen, the

compound must be either .... or in .... Electrolysis can occur when an electric ....

passes through a molten .... The two rods dipping into the electrolyte are called the ....

In this situation, metals are deposited at the .... and non-metals are formed at the ....

When the ionic compound is dissolved in water, the electrolysis can be more complex. Generally, during

electrolysis .... ions move towards the .... and negative ions move towards

the .... At the negative electrode (cathode) the metal or .... ions gain electrons and

form metal atoms or hydrogen .... At the positive electrode (anode) certain non-metal

ions .... electrons and .... or chlorine is produced.

b Complete the passage by using the words listed below.

hydrogen	hydroxide	lower	copper	sodium
cryolite	purifying	positive	concentrated	molten

Examples of electrolysis in industry

There are several important industrial applications of electrolysis, the most important economically being

the electrolysis of .... aluminium oxide to produce aluminium. The aluminium oxide is mixed with

olten .... to .... the melting point of the electrolyte.

A .... aqueous solution of sodium chloride contains ...., chloride, hydrogen and

.... ions. When this solution is electrolysed .... rather than sodium is discharged at the

negative electrode. The solution remaining is sodium hydroxide.

When a solution of copper(II) sulfate is electrolysed using .... electrodes, an unusual thing happens

and the copper atoms of the .... electrode (anode) go into solution as copper ions. At the cathode the

copper ions turn into copper atoms, and the metal is deposited on this electrode. This can be used as a method of

refining or .... impure copper.

Exercise C4.04 Displacement reactions of the halogens

> This exercise will build your understanding of a certain type of reaction and help improve your skills in organising and presenting experimental observations.

The halogens – chlorine, bromine and iodine – differ in terms of their ability to displace another halogen from a solution of its salt. The following are some notes from a students experiment. They include some rough observations from the tests carried out.

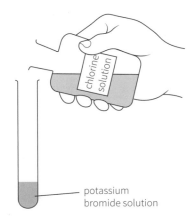

The halogens were provided as solutions in water and the test was to add the halogen to the salt solution. Solutions of potassium chloride, potassium bromide and potassium iodide were provided (see diagram).

To add further observations, hexane was also available as a solvent to mix with the reaction mixture at the end of the experiment. If there appeared to be a reaction, the product was shaken with hexane and the layers allowed to separate. The colour, if any, of the hexane layer was noted.

Results

Rough notes:

1 KCl solution with bromine or iodine solutions – no change to courless solution – hexane not added.

2 KBr solution with iodine solution – no change to colourless solution – hexane not added.

3 KBr solution, with chlorine solution – solution colourless to brown – brown colour moves to upper hexane layer at end.

4 KI solution with chlorine or bromine water – solution colourless to brown, in both cases – purple colour in upper hexane layer at end (brown colour of aqueous layer reduced).

a Take these recorded observations and draw up a table of the results. If there is no change, then write 'no reaction'.

Use this checklist to give yourself a mark for your results table. For each point, award yourself:
- **2 marks if you did it really well**
- **1 mark if you made a good attempt at it, and partly succeeded**
- **0 marks if you did not try to do it, or did not succeed.**

Self-assessment checklist for results tables:

Check point	Marks awarded	
	You	Your teacher
You have drawn the table with a ruler.		
The headings are appropriate and cover the observations you expect to make.		
The observations are recorded accurately, clearly and concisely – without over-elaboration.		
The table is easy for someone else to read and understand.		
Total (out of 8)		

8	Excellent.
7	Good.
5–6	A good start, but you need to improve quite a bit.
3–4	Poor. Try this same results table again, using a new sheet of paper.
1–2	Very poor. Read through all the criteria again, and then try the same results table again.

b Use the results to complete the diagram below which places the halogens tested in order of increasing reactivity.

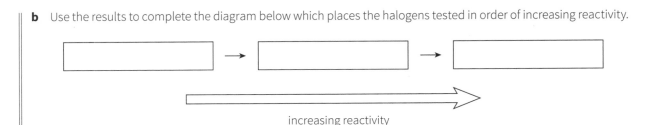

increasing reactivity

Exercise C4.05 Self-heating cans, hand warmers and cool packs

> Chemical reactions involve energy changes and this fact can be exploited for a range of practical purposes. This exercise illustrates those purposes and introduces aspects of exothermic and endothermic reactions which will also be met in later chapters.

Self-heating cans

Drinks, soups and other foods can be purchased in self-heating cans. Such containers are particularly useful on expeditions and in circumstances where transportation space is restricted.

These cans rely on a chemical reaction that produces sufficient heat to raise the temperature of the drink or food that surrounds the reaction vessel. The most common reaction used is the reaction between calcium oxide (slaked lime) and water. When this reaction takes place, a great deal of heat is given off and the solid calcium oxide swells to occupy a greater volume.

The diagram shows one way in which such a can may be constructed.

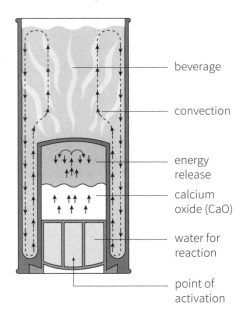

- beverage

- convection

- energy release

- calcium oxide (CaO)

- water for reaction

- point of activation

a What term is used for a reaction that gives out heat to the external surroundings?

....

b What problem might arise because of the expansion of the solid when water is added?

....

c Look carefully at the diagram and suggest how this problem might be overcome.

....

d Write the word and balanced chemical equations for the reaction between calcium oxide and water.

....

....

e How is calcium oxide manufactured from limestone?

....

....

f Using the internet, find **two** other exothermic reactions that are used in self-heating cans.

....

....

Heat pads and hand warmers

Some reactions are not obviously exothermic but have uses in this context. For example, the rusting reaction of iron generates heat for several hours and is used in pocket hand warmers (see diagram) for expeditions to cold regions. It is also used in the heat pads employed in first aid to relieve the aches and pains caused by strain in muscles and joints.

a The heat pad contains iron powder and water absorbed within the pad. While sealed, the rusting reaction cannot take place. What further reactant is needed which only comes into play when the sealed packaging is opened?

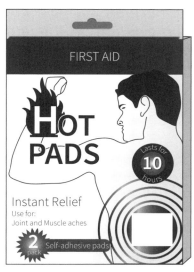

....

....

b Rust is hydrated iron(III) oxide. What is the chemical formula of iron(III) oxide?

....

....

c Complete the equation for the formation of rust.

$$\text{.......} Fe + \text{.......} O_2 + 2xH_2O \longrightarrow \text{.......} Fe_2O_3 \cdot xH_2O$$

d The pad also contains salt. Why is this present as a component of the reacting mixture?

....

....

e Hand warmers can be made using a solution of sodium thiosulfate which contains more than the normal amount of the salt that can be dissolved at room temperature. A metallic clicker' is used to create a physical disturbance in the solution and the excess salt crystallises out, releasing a substantial amount of heat.

    i What is the term used for such a solution that contains more dissolved solute than is normal?

    ....

    ii How can such a hand warmer be re-used after the salt has been crystallised out?

    ....

    ....

    iii Is a hand warmer based on the rusting reaction re-usable? Explain your answer.

    ....

    ....

Cool packs

Reactions that absorb heat from the surroundings are also of use in circumstances where things needed to be cooled down or kept cool. There are two types of cool pack:

• Instant cool packs that contain a solid which dissolves endothermically in water that is kept separate from the solid in the package until needed.

• Cool packs that contain a gel which is cooled down in a freezer and which warms up slowly when removed (see diagram). This type of cool pack can be re-used.

Instant cool packs usually contain crystals of ammonium nitrate together with a plastic bag of water which is burst to activate the pack.

a Give another use for ammonium nitrate.

....

b Give **one** advantage and **one** disadvantage of this type of cool pack

Advantage:

....

Disadvantage:

....

c Cool packs can be used to keep vaccines and other medicines cool in hot climates. A temperature of 5 °C is usually required. Devise an experiment to discover how much ammonium nitrate and how much water would have to be used to produce the temperature of 5 °C needed to keep a vaccine cool in hot desert conditions.

....

....

....

....

....

Exercise C4.06 The movement of ions

This exercise introduces the idea of the movement of ions in an electrical field and the basis of the terms 'anion' and 'cation'.

A student set up an experiment like this to look at the movement of ions. The filter paper is damp and a small crystal of the solid being studied is placed in the centre as shown in the diagram.

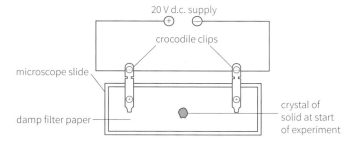

The results are shown in Table 4.03

Substance	Colour of crystals	Changes seen on the filter paper
potassium manganate(VII), $KMnO_4$	purple	purple colour moves towards positive
potassium sulfate, K_2SO_4	white	no colours seen
copper sulfate, $CuSO_4$	blue	blue colour moves towards negative

Table 4.03

a Which of these ions is yellow?

manganate   copper   potassium   sulfate

....

b Explain why the purple colour moves towards the positive terminal in the potassium manganate experiment.

....

....

c List the anions and cations involved in this experiment, together with their formulae.

Anions:

....

Cations:

....

d Suggest and explain what will happen if this experiment is repeated with a crystal of copper manganate(VII).

....

....

....

....

Exercise C4.07 Making and 'breaking' copper chloride

> The difference between synthesis and decomposition is emphasised in this exercise together with a consideration of the energy changes involved.

'Dutch metal' is a form of brass containing a very high proportion of copper. It is generally used as very thin sheets for gilding, as imitation gold leaf.

Synthesising copper(II) chloride

a What are the words we use to describe a metal that can be drawn out and beaten into thin sheets?

....

The following is a description of the reaction of Dutch metal with chlorine gas to produce copper(II) chloride.

A clean dry gas jar is filled with chlorine gas in a fume cupboard. The lid of the gas jar is lifted and two thin sheets of Dutch metal are lowered into the gas using tongs. The lid is quickly replaced.

A flash of flame is observed and clouds of yellow 'smoke' are formed.

A small volume of distilled water is added to the gas jar and shaken to dissolve the smoke. A pale blue-green (turquoise) solution is formed.

b What colour is chlorine gas?

....

c Why is the reaction carried out in a fume cupboard?

....

d Is the reaction observed exothermic or endothermic? What feature of Dutch metal helps the reaction take place quickly? Explain your answers.

....

....

....

e What observation indicates that the solution obtained contains copper(II) chloride?

....

f Give the chemical equation for the synthesis reaction that has taken place.

....

g Dutch metal is an alloy of copper (84%) and zinc (16%). What other salt may be present in the solution?

....

Decomposing copper(II) chloride

Copper(II) chloride can be decomposed to its elements by electrolysis. A simple cell such as the one shown in the diagram below can be set up so that the chlorine gas can be collected.

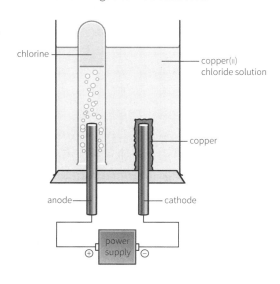

a Write word and symbol equations for the overall reaction taking place during this electrolysis.

....

....

b Define the term 'electrolysis'.

....

....

....

c How would you test the gas collected at the anode to show that it was chlorine?

....

....

d A much simpler set of apparatus can be used to show this electrolysis. This is shown in the diagram below.

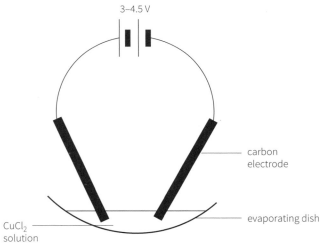

i If this simpler apparatus is used, where must the electrolysis be carried out for safety reasons?

....

ii Using this simple apparatus, there is no collection of any gas produced. How could you test to show that chlorine had been produced in this case? Explain why it would work.

....

....

....

e Is the decomposition of copper(II) chloride exothermic or endothermic? What type of energy is involved in this reaction?

....

....

f Write the half-equations for the reactions taking place at the anode (positive electrode) and the cathode (negative electrode).

At the anode:

....

At the cathode:

....

Chapter C5
Acids, bases and salts

KEY TERMS

acid: a substance that dissolves in water to give a solution with a pH below 7

base: a substance which will neutralise an acid to give a salt and water only

alkali: a base that dissolves in water

pH scale: a measure of the acidity or alkalinity of a solution (scale from 0 to 14)

indicator: a substance that changes colour depending on whether it is in an acid or alkali

salt: an ionic substance produced from an acid by neutralisation with a base

neutralisation: reaction a reaction between an acid and a base to produce a salt and water only

USEFUL REACTIONS AND THEIR EQUATIONS

Neutralisation reactions

$HCl(aq) + NaOH(aq) \longrightarrow NaCl(aq) + H_2O(l)$

$H_2SO_4(aq) + 2KOH(aq) \longrightarrow K_2SO_4(aq) + 2H_2O(l)$

$CuO(s) + H_2SO_4(aq) \longrightarrow CuSO_4(aq) + H_2O(l)$

Other characteristic acid reactions

$CaCO_3(s) + 2HCl(aq) \longrightarrow CaCl_2(aq) + CO_2(g) + H_2O(l)$

$CuCO_3(s) + H_2SO_4(aq) \longrightarrow CuSO_4(aq) + CO_2(g) + H_2O(l)$

$Zn(s) + H_2SO_4(aq) \longrightarrow ZnSO_4(aq) + H_2(g)$

$Mg(s) + 2HCl(aq) \longrightarrow MgCl_2(aq) + H_2(g)$

Exercise C5.01 Acid and base reactions – neutralisation

> This exercise will help you familiarise yourself with some of the terms involved in talking about acids and bases.

Choose words from the list below to fill in the gaps in the following statements.

acid	carbon dioxide	hydrogen	hydrated	anhydrous
metal	sodium	sulfuric	water	

All salts are ionic compounds. Salts are produced when an alkali neutralises an .... In this reaction, the salt is formed when a .... ion or an ammonium ion from the alkali replaces one or more .... ions of the acid.

Salts can be crystallised from the solution produced by the neutralisation reaction. The salt crystals formed often contain .... of crystallisation. These salts are called .... salts. The salt crystals can be heated to drive off the .... of crystallisation. The salt remaining is said to be ....

Salts can be made by other reactions of acids. Magnesium sulfate can be made by reacting magnesium carbonate with .... acid. The gas given off is .... Water is also formed in this reaction.

All .... salts are soluble in water.

Exercise C5.02 Types of salt

This exercise aims to increase your confidence in predicting the products of the characteristic reactions of acids, particularly in terms of naming the salt produced in a reaction.

Salts are produced in reactions where the hydrogen of an acid is replaced by metal ions or the ammonium ion. Each acid gives a characteristic family of salts. Sulfuric acid, for instance, always produces sulfates.

a Complete the following statements for other acids.

   i   Hydrochloric acid always produces ....

   ii Nitric acid always produces ....

   iii Ethanoic acid always produces ....

b Complete Table 5.01 which summarises the products of various reactions of acids.

Substances reacted together		Salt produced	Other products of the reaction
dilute hydrochloric acid	zinc oxide		
dilute sulfuric acid		copper sulfate	water and carbon dioxide
		magnesium sulfate	water and carbon dioxide
		magnesium chloride	hydrogen
dilute hydrochloric acid	copper oxide		
dilute ethanoic acid		sodium ethanoate	water

Table 5.01

Exercise C5.03 Antacids

This exercise discusses the different compounds that we can use to counteract the effects of acid indigestion. The reactions involved with the different remedies are considered.

The human stomach contains hydrochloric acid with a pH of about 2. This plays a part in the process by which we digest our food. Acid indigestion (heartburn) is due to the stomach producing too much hydrochloric acid. This causes discomfort and often pain.

One way to deal with this is to take an antacid. Antacids (shown in the diagram below) contain chemicals which react with and neutralise the acid in the stomach.

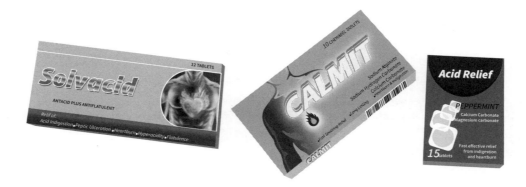

Below are listed a number of common ingredients of antacid remedies:

- sodium carbonate

- sodium hydrogencarbonate

- calcium carbonate

- magnesium carbonate

- magnesium hydroxide

- aluminium hydroxide

- sodium alginate.

a Write equations showing the reactions between magnesium carbonate and magnesium hydroxide with hydrochloric acid.

i $MgCO_3$

....

ii $Mg(OH)_2$

....

b Why might the reaction with magnesium carbonate cause some discomfort?

....

c Some of the compounds listed earlier are soluble in water,

   i Which **two** compounds are soluble in water?

   ....

   ii Why might these compounds work more quickly?

   ....

   ....

d Sodium alginate does not neutralise acid. Use the internet to find why it is used in antacids.

   ....

   ....

   ....

Exercise C5.04 Fire extinguishers

Carbon dioxide is often used in fire extinguishers. This exercise describes a traditional 'wet' carbon dioxide extinguisher, and discusses the different types of extinguisher and their appropriate use. You can use the internet to research other types of fire extinguisher.

The diagram shows an early type of fire extinguisher. The extinguisher was turned upside down, causing the stopper to come out of the acid bottle.

The reaction between acid and carbonate then produced a mixture of water and carbon dioxide which was squirted at the fire. It was important that a large volume of carbon dioxide was produced quickly.

This type of extinguisher is not suitable for all types of fire.

It is possible to use sodium hydrogencarbonate instead of sodium carbonate and hydrochloric acid instead of sulfuric acid.

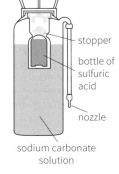

stopper

bottle of sulfuric acid

nozzle

sodium carbonate solution

a Below are the equations for the possible reactions:

   1 $Na_2CO_3 + H_2SO_4 \rightarrow Na_2SO_4 + H_2O + CO_2$

   2 $Na_2CO_3 + 2HCl \rightarrow 2NaCl + H_2O + CO_2$

   3 $2NaHCO_3 + H_2SO_4 \rightarrow Na_2SO_4 + 2H_2O + 2CO_2$

   4 $NaHCO_3 + HCl \rightarrow NaCl + H_2O + CO_2$

Answer the following questions, assuming that all four solutions are of the same concentration and in equal volumes.

   i Which combination(s) would produce carbon dioxide most quickly? Explain your answer.

   Combination (3) because the two moles of carbon dioxide are produced for each mole of acid.

   ....

ii Which combination(s) would produce least carbon dioxide? Explain your answer.

Combination (2) because there are two moles of acid while there is only one mole of carbon dioxide

b Use the internet to discover what types of fire extinguisher are used now. Comment on the type(s) of fire they are useful for and the types they are not.

– Water extinguishers are used for organic materials such as paper fabrics and wood. It has the cooling effect on the fuel, causing it to burn much more slowly until the flames are eventually extinguished.
– Foam extinguishers are also used for organic materials. It has the same effect as water, creating a barrier between the flame and the fuel

c Which extinguisher is sometimes called the 'universal extinguisher' and why?

Dry powder extinguishers because they can be used for all all types of fire. It is safe in most of cases

Exercise C5.05 Descaling a coffee machine

The formation of limescale in coffee makers, kettles and hot water pipes is a problem in certain areas. This exercise considers various acids that are used to remove limescale and their effectiveness.

Coffee makers (see diagram, previous page) can become blocked with 'limescale' in hard water areas. Limescale is calcium carbonate which precipitates from the hot water in the machine and blocks the pipes.

It is often necessary to 'descale' the machines. This is done by passing acid through the pipes. The acid reacts with the calcium carbonate and so removes it.

The following acids have been used for descaling:

- hydrochloric acid

- citric acid

- ethanoic acid (vinegar)

- sulfamic acid.

a Write word and symbol equations for the reaction between calcium carbonate and hydrochloric acid.

Calcium carbonate + hydrochloric acid → Calcium chloride + water

$CaCO_3 + 2HCl \rightarrow CaCl_2 + H_2O + CO_2$ + carbon dioxide

b What name would be given to the salt formed when citric acid reacts with calcium carbonate?

Calcium citrate

c Why might these acids not be the best to use for descaling a coffee machine?

i Hydrochloric acid

Hydrochloric acid is a strong acid that might cause reaction with metal

ii Ethanoic acid

Ethanoic acid has a taste of vinegar that might affect the coffee.

d Search the internet to find the answers to the following questions.

i What is the formula of sulfamic acid and what is it used for?

H_3NSO_3 is frequently used for removing rust and limescale.

ii Why does water sometimes produce calcium carbonate (limescale) when it is heated? What is hard water?

Hard water is water that has high mineral content. Hard water is formed when water percolates through deposits of limestone and chalk which are largely made up of calcium and magnesium carbonates. When water is boiled in a kettle, limescale that lurks inside your kettle and stains your surface.

Exercise C5.06 The analysis of titration results

> This exercise will develop your understanding of some of the practical skills involved in acid–base titrations and the processing and evaluation of experimental results.

A student investigated an aqueous solution of sodium hydroxide and its reaction with hydrochloric acid. He carried out two experiments.

Experiment 1

Using a measuring cylinder, 10 cm³ of the sodium hydroxide solution was placed in a conical flask. Methyl orange indicator was added to the flask. A burette was filled to the 0.0 cm³ mark with hydrochloric acid (solution **P**).

The student added solution **P** slowly to the alkali in the flask until the colour just changed. Use the burette diagram to record the volume in the results table and complete the column for Experiment **1** in Table 5.02.

Experiment 2

Experiment **1** was repeated using a different solution of hydrochloric acid (solution **Q**). Use the burette diagrams to record the volumes and complete the Experiment **2** column in Table 5.02.

Table of results

Burette readings / cm³	Experiment 1	Experiment 2
final reading		
initial reading	0.0	
difference		

Table 5.02

a What type of chemical reaction occurs when hydrochloric acid reacts with sodium hydroxide?

....

b Write a word equation for the reaction.

....

c What was the colour change of the indicator observed?

....

d Which of the experiments used the greater volume of hydrochloric acid?

....

56

e Compare the volumes of acid used in Experiments **1** and **2** and suggest an explanation for the difference between the volumes.

....

....

f Predict the volume of hydrochloric acid **P** that would be needed to react completely if Experiment **1** was repeated with 25 cm³ of sodium hydroxide solution.

Volume of solution needed: ....

Explanation

....

g Suggest **one** change the student could make to the **apparatus** used in order to obtain more accurate results.

....

Exercise 5.07 Thermochemistry – investigating the neutralisation of an acid by an alkali

> **This exercise introduces an unfamiliar form of titration and further develops your skills in presenting, processing and evaluating the results of practical work.**

The reaction between dilute nitric acid and dilute sodium hydroxide solutions can be investigated by thermochemistry. This can be done by following the changes in temperature as one solution is added to another.

Apparatus

- polystyrene cup and beaker
- 25 cm³ measuring cylinder
- 100 cm³ measuring cylinder
- thermometer (0 to 100 °C)

safety glasses – to be used when handling the acid and alkali solutions

Method

An experiment was carried out to measure the temperature changes during the neutralisation of sodium hydroxide solution with dilute nitric acid. Both solutions were allowed to stand in the laboratory for about 30 min.

25 cm³ of sodium hydroxide solution was added to a polystyrene beaker and the temperature was measured.

Then 10 cm³ of nitric acid was added to the alkali in the beaker and the highest temperature reached was measured.

The experiment was repeated using the following volumes of acid: 20, 30, 40, 50 and 60 cm³.

Results

Temperature of alkali solution at start of experiment = 21.0 °C.

The following temperatures were obtained for the different volumes of added acid used: 28.0, 35.0, 35.0, 31.0, 30.0 and 27.5 °C respectively.

a Record these results here in a suitable table.

Use this checklist to give yourself a mark for your results table. For each point, award yourself:

- **2 marks if you did it really well**
- **1 mark if you made a good attempt at it, and partly succeeded**
- **0 marks if you did not try to do it, or did not succeed.**

Self-assessment checklist for results tables:

Check point	Marks awarded	
	You	**Your teacher**
You have drawn the table with a ruler.		
The headings are appropriate and have the correct units in each column/row.		
The table is easy for someone else to read and understand.		
If the table contains readings, all are to the same number of decimal places (e.g. 15.5, 14.2, etc.).		
Total (out of 8)		

8	Excellent.
7	Good.
5–6	A good start, but you need to improve quite a bit.
3–4	Poor. Try this same results table again, using a new sheet of paper.
1–2	Very poor. Read through all the criteria again, and then try the same results table again.

b Plot a graph of the temperature of the solution against the volume of acid added to the alkali.

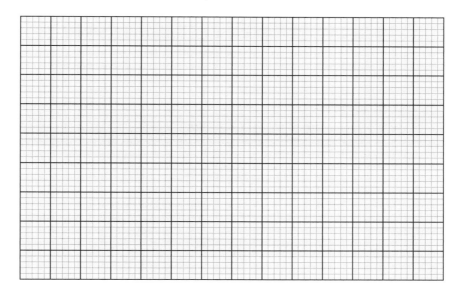

c Draw suitable lines through the points on your graph. (Note that there are two parts to this graph so you will need to draw **two** straight lines through the points and extend them until they cross.)

d Which point appears to be inaccurate?

....

e From these results work out the volume of acid needed to neutralise 25 cm³ of the sodium hydroxide solution. Explain why you have chosen this value.

....

....

Use the checklist below to give yourself a mark for your graph. For each point, award yourself:

- 2 marks if you did it really well
- 1 mark if you made a good attempt at it, and partly succeeded
- 0 marks if you did not try to do it, or did not succeed.

Self-assessment checklist for graphs:

Check point	Marks awarded	
	You	Your teacher
You have drawn the axes with a ruler, using most of the width and height of the grid.		
You have used a good scale for the *x*-axis and the *y*-axis, going up in 1 s, 2 s, 5 s or 10 s.		
You have labelled the axes correctly, giving the correct units for the scales on both axes.		
You have plotted each point precisely and correctly.		
You have used a small, neat cross for each point.		
You have drawn a single, clear best-fit line through each set of points – using a ruler for straight lines – and have extended the lines to meet.		
You have ignored any anomalous results when drawing the lines.		
Total (out of 14)		

12–14   Excellent.

10–11   Good.

7–9   A good start, but you need to improve quite a bit.

5–6   Poor. Try this same graph again, using a new sheet of graph paper.

1–4   Very poor. Read through all the criteria again, and then try the same graph again.

f   Why were the solutions left to stand for about 30 min before the experiments?

....

g   Why was a polystyrene beaker used instead of a glass beaker?

....

h   Suggest **three** improvements that would make the experiment more accurate.

....

....

....

i Write the word equation and balanced chemical equation for the reaction.

....

....

j Is the reaction exothermic or endothermic? ....

k The concentration of the sodium hydroxide solution is 1.0 mol/dm³. How many moles are there in 25 cm³ of this solution? (Remember there are 1000 cm³ in 1 dm³.)

....

l Look at the equation and work out how many moles of nitric acid this would react with.

....

m Calculate how many moles of acid there are in 1000 cm³ of the acid solution. What is the concentration of the acid solution in mol/dm³?

....

relative atomic mass: the average mass of naturally occurring atoms of an element on a scale where the carbon-12 atom has a mass of exactly 12 units

relative formula mass: the sum of all the relative atomic masses of all the atoms or ions in a compound

mole: the relative formula mass of a substance in grams

molar gas volume: the volume occupied by 1 mole of any gas (24 dm³ at room temperature and pressure)

Exercise C6.01 Calculating formula masses

> **This exercise will develop your understanding and recall of the ideas about atomic and formula mass.**

a   Complete the following diagram by filling in the blanks.

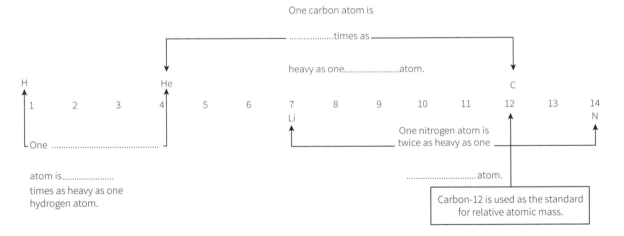

b Complete Table 6.01 of formula masses for a range of different types of substance. (Relative atomic masses: O = 16, H = 1, C = 12, N = 14, Ca = 40, Mg = 24.)

Molecule	Chemical formula	Number of atoms or ions involved	Relative formula mass
oxygen	O_2	2 O	$2 \times 16 = 32$
carbon dioxide	....	1 C and 2 O	$1 \times 12 + 2 \times 16 =$ ....
....	H_2O	2 H and 1	.... = ...
ammonia	....	1 N and 3 H	.... = ...
calcium carbonate	....	1 Ca^{2+} and 1 CO_3^{2-}	.... + ... + $3 \times 16 = 100$
....	MgO	1 Mg^{2+} and 1 O^{2-}	$1 \times 24 + 1 \times 16 =$ ....
ammonium nitrate	NH_4NO_3	1 NH_4^+ and	$2 \times 14 +$ .... + ... = 80
propanol	C_3H_7OH	3 C, ... and	$3 \times 12 + 8 \times 1 +$ .... = ...

Table 6.01

Exercise C6.02 A sense of proportion in chemistry

> This exercise will familiarise you with some of the basic calculations involved in chemistry.

a Zinc metal is extracted from its oxide. In the industrial extraction process, 5 tonnes of zinc oxide are needed to produce 4 tonnes of zinc. Calculate the mass of zinc, in tonnes, that is produced from 20 tonnes of zinc oxide.

b Nitrogen and hydrogen react together to form ammonia

$$N_2 + 3H_2 \longrightarrow 2NH_3$$

When the reaction is complete, 14 tonnes of nitrogen are converted into 17 tonnes of ammonia. How much nitrogen will be needed to produce 34 tonnes of ammonia?

c The sugar lactose, $C_{12}H_{22}O_{11}$, is sometimes used in place of charcoal in fireworks.

State the total number of atoms present in a molecule of lactose ....

d A molecule of compound **Y** contains the following atoms bonded covalently together:

- two atoms of carbon (C)

- two atoms of oxygen (O)

- four atoms of hydrogen (H).

What is the formula of a molecule of **Y**? ....

Exercise C6.03 Calculations involving solutions

This exercise will help develop your understanding of the idea of the mole and its application to the concentration of solutions. It will develop your skills in processing practical data from titrations.

Testing the purity of citric acid

Citric acid is an organic acid which is a white solid at room temperature. It dissolves readily in water.

The purity of a sample of the acid was tested by the following method.

- Step 1: A sample of 0.48 g citric acid was dissolved in 50 cm³ of distilled water.

- Step 2: Drops of thymolphthalein indicator were added (colour change is from colourless in acid to blue in alkali).

- Step 3: The solution was then titrated with a solution of sodium hydroxide (0.50 mol/dm³).

a i Complete the labels for the pieces of apparatus shown in the diagram below and give the colour of the solution before titration.

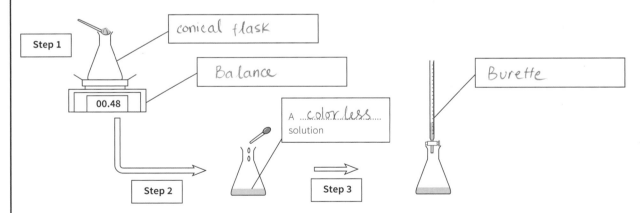

ii Table 6.02 shows the burette readings from the titration. Complete the table by filling in the missing value (*P*).

Final burette reading / cm³	14.60
First burette reading / cm³	0.20
Volume of NaOH(aq) added / cm³	......14.40.........(P)

Table 6.02

b Calculate the purity of the citric acid by following the stages outlined here.

Stage 1: Calculate the number of moles of alkali solution reacted in the titration.

- P cm³ of NaOH(aq) containing 0.50 moles in 1000 cm³ were used.

- Number of moles NaOH used $= \dfrac{0.50}{1000} \times P = Q =$ .....7.20×10^{-3}..... moles.

Stage 2: Calculate the number of moles of citric acid in the sample.

- Note that 1 mole of citric acid reacts with 3 moles of sodium hydroxide.

- Then number of moles of citric acid in sample $= \dfrac{Q}{3} = R =$ .....0.0024....... moles.

Stage 3: Calculate the mass of citric acid in the sample and therefore the percentage purity.

- Relative formula mass of citric acid (M_r of $C_6H_8O_7$) = ...192...............
  (C = 12; H = 1; O = 16)

- Mass of citric acid in sample $= R \times M_r = S =$ ......0.46.......... g.

- Percentage purity of sample $= \dfrac{S}{0.48} =$ ....95.8......... %.

c How could the sample of citric acid be purified further?

........The sample of citric acid could be purified further by........

re - crytalisation..................

Exercise C6.04 Finding the mass of 5 cm of magnesium ribbon

> **This exercise will develop your skills in handling experimental data in novel situations.**

From the chemical equation for the reaction and using the relative formula masses together with the molar volume of a gas it is possible to predict the amounts of magnesium sulfate and hydrogen that are produced when 24 g of magnesium are reacted with excess sulfuric acid.

This relationship between the mass of magnesium used and the volume of gas produced can be used to find the mass of a short piece of magnesium ribbon indirectly.

Apparatus and method

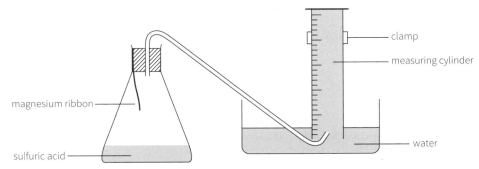

The experimental instructions were as follows.

Wear safety goggles for eye protection.

- Set up the apparatus as shown in the diagram with 25 cm³ of sulfuric acid in the flask.

- Make sure the measuring cylinder is completely full of water.

- Carefully measure 5 cm of magnesium ribbon and grip it below the flask stopper as shown.

- Ease the stopper up to release the ribbon and immediately replace it.

- When no further bubbles rise into the measuring cylinder, record the volume of gas collected.

- Repeat the experiment twice more using 5 cm of magnesium ribbon and fresh sulfuric acid each time.

- Find the average volume of hydrogen produced.

Data handling

A student obtained the results shown in Table 6.03 when measuring the volume of hydrogen produced.

Experiment number	Volume of hydrogen collected / cm³
1	85
2	79
3	82
average	82

Table 6.03

a Fill in the average of the results obtained. Can you think of possible reasons why the three results are not the same?

<u>The size of magnesium ribbon may not be the same</u>

b You know that 24 g of magnesium will produce 24 000 cm³ of hydrogen. What mass of magnesium would be needed to produce your volume of hydrogen?

$$24 g \rightarrow 24000 \, cm^3$$
$$? \, g \rightarrow 82 \, cm^3$$

$$\text{Mass of magnesium} = \frac{82 \times 24}{24000}$$
$$= 0.082 \, g$$

This is the mass of 5 cm of magnesium ribbon. The weight is too low to weigh easily on a balance but you could weigh a longer length and use that to check your answer.

c What mass of magnesium sulfate would you expect 5 cm of magnesium ribbon to produce?

$$24g \, Mg \rightarrow 120 \, g \, MgSO_4$$
$$0.082g \rightarrow \, ?$$

$$0.082 \times 120 \div 24 = 0.41g$$

d Plan an experiment to check whether your prediction above is correct.

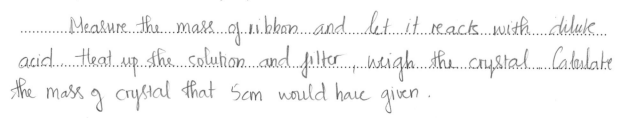

Measure the mass of ribbon and let it reacts with dilute acid. Heat up the solution and filter, weigh the crystal. Calculate the mass of crystal that 5cm would have given.

Exercise C6.05 Reacting volumes of gases

There is a direct relationship between the volume of a gas and the number of moles present in the sample. This exercise gives you an example of how to use that relationship for a particular experiment.

Experiments show that volumes of gases react together in a ratio that can be predicted from the chemical equation for the reaction.

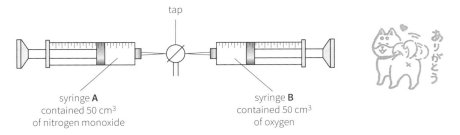

tap

syringe **A**
contained 50 cm³
of nitrogen monoxide

syringe **B**
contained 50 cm³
of oxygen

Under the conditions as shown in the diagram, nitrogen monoxide (NO) reacts with oxygen (O) to form one product that is a brown gas. In an experiment, 5.0 cm³ portions of oxygen were pushed from syringe **B** into syringe **A**.

After each addition, the tap was closed, the gases were cooled, and then the total volume of gases remaining was measured. The results are shown in the graph.

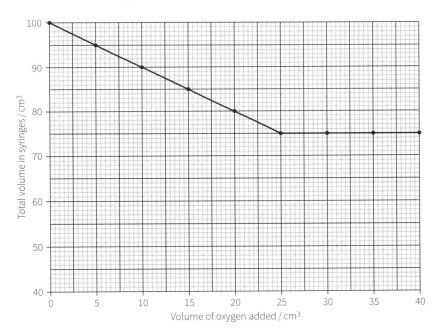

a What is the total volume of gases when the reaction is complete?

.... 75 cm³ ....

b What volume of oxygen reacts with 50 cm³ of nitrogen monoxide?

.... 25 cm³ ....

c What is the volume of the brown gas formed?

$50 cm^3$

d Complete the following to work out the formula of the brown gas:

2 NO $+$ O_2 $\rightarrow$ 2 NO_2
50 cm³ 25 cm³ 50 cm³

Exercise C6.06 Calculation triangles

The conversion of the mass of a sample into moles and vice versa is central to chemical calculations because it gives us a measure of the number of atoms and/or molecules involved in reactions. This exercise will help you become familiar with the use of the calculation 'triangles' that are a memory aid to these conversions.

a Converting masses to moles, and moles to masses

Fill in the calculation triangle in the diagram below for changing between masses and moles. Then complete Table 6.04. (Use the following A_r values: H = 1, C = 12, N = 14, O = 16, Mg = 24, S = 32, Cl = 35.5, Ca = 40, Cu = 64.)

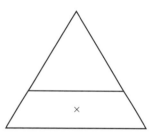

Substance	A_r or M_r	Number of moles	Mass / g
Cu			128
Mg		0.5	
Cl_2			35.5
H_2			4
S_8		2	
O_3			1.6
H_2SO_4		2.5	
CO_2		0.4	
NH_3			25.5
$CaCO_3$			100
$MgSO_4 \cdot 7H_2O$			82

Table 6.04

b Calculations involving solutions

Fill in the calculation triangle in the diagram below for relating moles of solute to volume and concentration. Then complete Table 6.05 below.

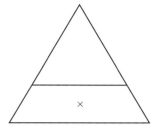

Solute	Volume of solution	Concentration of solution / mol/dm³	Moles of solute present
sodium chloride	1 dm³	0.5	
hydrochloric acid	500 cm³	0.5	
sodium hydroxide	2 dm³		1
sulfuric acid	250 cm³		0.5
sodium thiosulfate		2	0.4
copper(II) sulfate		0.1	0.75

Table 6.05

Exercise C6.07 Scaling up!

One aspect of carrying out calculations in chemistry is the scaling up of the amounts used to industrial proportions. This exercise gives you some practice at this skill.

In the laboratory we are used to working with grams of material and our calculations are usually framed on that basis. However, an industrial chemist is often used to working on a significantly larger scale and looking to produce tonnes of product.

a In this context, it is useful to know that the reacting proportions determined by the equation for the reaction can be readily scaled up to provide useful data at an industrial level.

i What mass of iron(III) oxide is needed to produce 100 g of iron, in the blast furnace? Complete the sentence below using your calculated figures. (Use the following A_r values: C = 12; O = 16; Fe = 56.)

The equation for the reaction is:

$Fe_2O_3(s) + 3CO(g) \rightarrow 2Fe(s) + 3CO_2(g)$

69

100 g of iron is .... moles of Fe, so .... moles of Fe_2O_3 are needed for the reaction,

or .... g of iron(III) oxide.

ii   Using your calculated value for how much iron(III) oxide (hematite) is needed to produce 100 g of iron, state how much hematite is needed to produce 50 tonnes of iron.

....

....

b   Another large-scale industrial process is the production of quicklime from limestone by heating in a lime kiln.

i   What is the equation for the thermal decomposition of limestone?

....

ii   Using your equation, calculate how many tonnes of quicklime would be produced from 1 tonne of limestone. (A_r of Ca = 40.)

....

....

....

Chapter C7
How far? How fast?

KEY TERMS

exothermic reaction: a reaction that gives out heat to the surroundings

endothermic reaction: a reaction that takes in heat from the surroundings

rate of reaction: the rate of formation of the products of a chemical reaction (or the rate at which the reactants are used up)

catalyst: a substance that speeds up a chemical reaction but remains unchanged at the end of the reaction

enzyme: a protein that functions as a biological catalyst

activation energy: the minimum amount of energy the reacting molecules must have for a reaction to take place

USEFUL REACTIONS AND THEIR EQUATIONS

These reactions are often used to study reaction rates or are useful examples of reversible reactions:

$Mg + 2HCl \longrightarrow MgCl_2 + H_2$

$CaCO_3 + 2HCl \longrightarrow CaCl_2 + H_2O + CO_2$

$CuSO_4 + 5H_2O \rightleftharpoons CuSO_4 \cdot 5H_2O$

$2H_2O_2(l) \rightleftharpoons 2H_2O(l) + O_2(g)$

$Na_2S_2O_3(aq) + 2HCl(aq) \longrightarrow 2NaCl(aq) + SO_2(g) + H_2O(l) + S(s)$

$N_2 + 3H_2 \rightleftharpoons 2NH_3$

$2SO_2(g) + O_2(g) \rightleftharpoons 2SO_3(g)$

Exercise C7.01 Terms of reaction

This exercise should help you familiarise yourself with certain key terms relating to the progress of chemical reactions.

Draw lines to match the terms on the left with the correct statement on the right.

Term	Statement
catalyst	a substance that speeds up a chemical reaction
exothermic reaction	the industrial process for making ammonia
reversible reaction	a reaction in which the products may react to produce the original reactants
Haber process	a reaction in which heat energy is given out to the surroundings
Contact process	the industrial process for making sulfuric acid

Exercise C7.02 Energy diagrams

This exercise is aimed at helping you understand energy level diagrams and their usefulness in showing why some reactions are exothermic while others are endothermic.

The energy changes involved in chemical reactions can be represented visually by energy level diagrams. Such diagrams show the relative stability of the reactants and products. The more stable a set of reactants or products, the lower their energy level.

The energy level diagram for an exothermic reaction is different from that for an endothermic reaction. The following keywords/phrases will be needed to fill in the information boxes accompanying the diagrams.

given out   **positive**   **taken in**   **reactants**   **negative**   **products**

a   Exothermic reactions

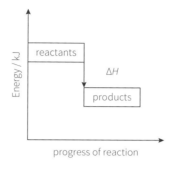

Use information from the diagram and the keywords/phrases to complete the following information box.

In an exothermic reaction, the .... have more energy than the ....

This means that ΔH is ....

The difference in energy is .... as heat.

The temperature of the surroundings ***increases / decreases***. (*Delete the incorrect word.*)

b   Endothermic reactions

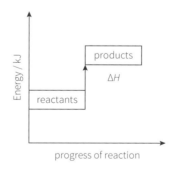

Again, use information from the diagram and the keywords/phrases to complete the following information box.

In an endothermic reaction, the .... have more energy than the ....

This means that ΔH is ....

The difference in energy is .... from the surroundings.

The temperature of the surroundings ***increases / decreases***. (*Delete the incorrect word.*)

73

Exercise C7.03 The collision theory of reaction rates

> This exercise should help you develop an understanding of the collision (particle) theory of reactions and how changing conditions affect the rate of various types of reaction.

Complete the Table 7.01 from your understanding of the factors that affect the speed (rate) of a reaction. Several of the sections have been completed already. The finished table should then be a useful revision aid.

Factor affecting the reaction	Types of reaction affected	Change made in the condition	Effect on rate of reaction
concentration	all reactions involving solutions or reactions involving gases	an increase in the concentration of one, or both, of the .... means there are more particles in the same volume	increases the rate of reaction as the particles .... more frequently
pressure	reactions involving .... only	an increase in the pressure	greatly .... the rate of reaction – the effect is the same as that of an increase in ....
temperature	all reactions	an increase in temperature – this means that molecules are moving .... and collide more ....; the particles also have more .... when they collide	.... the rate of reaction
particle size	reactions involving solids and liquids, solids and gases or mixtures of solids	use the same mass of a solid but make the pieces of solid	greatly increases the rate of reaction
using a catalyst	slow reactions can be speeded up by adding a suitable catalyst	reduces amount of .... required for the reaction to take place: the catalyst is present in the same .... at the end of the reaction	.... the rate of reaction

Table 7.01

Exercise C7.04 The influence of surface area on the rate of reaction

> This exercise should help develop your skills in presenting and manipulating experimental data. You will also be asked to interpret data and draw conclusions from it.

A useful experiment that shows the effect of varying the surface area of a solid on reaction rate is based on the fact that hydrochloric acid reacts with calcium carbonate to produce the gas carbon dioxide.

The experiment was set up as shown in the diagram below using identical masses of marble chips. Flask **A** contains larger pieces of marble chips and Flask **B** contains smaller pieces. The same concentration and volume of acid was used in both flasks.

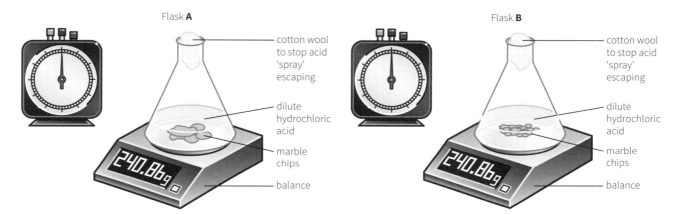

The flasks were quickly and simultaneously set to zero on the balances. The mass loss of the flasks was then recorded over time.

a Write the word equation for the reaction between marble chips (calcium carbonate) and dilute hydrochloric acid.

....

b What causes the loss in mass from the flasks?

....

....

Readings on the digital balance were taken every 30 s. The balance had been tared (set) to zero at the start of the reaction.

For the large pieces of marble chips (Flask **A**), readings (in g) were:

0.00	−0.21	−0.46	−0.65	−0.76	−0.81	−0.91
−0.92	−0.96	−0.98	−0.98	−1.00	−0.99	−0.99

For the small pieces of marble chips (Flask **B**), readings (in g) were:

0.00	−0.51	−0.78	−0.87	−0.91	−0.94	−0.96
−0.98	−0.99	−0.99	−0.99	−1.00	−0.99	−1.00

c Create a suitable table showing how the mass of carbon dioxide produced (equal to the loss of mass) varies with time for the two experiments.

d Plot the **two** graphs on the grid.

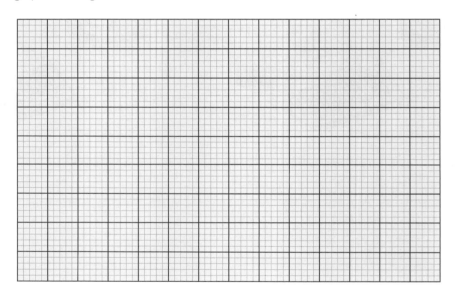

e Which pieces gave the faster rate of reaction? Explain why.

....

....

....

f Explain why for both flasks, the same amount of gas is produced in the end.

....

....

....

Use the checklist below to give yourself a mark for your graph. For each point, award yourself:
- 2 marks if you did it really well
- 1 mark if you made a good attempt at it, and partly succeeded
- 0 marks if you did not try to do it, or did not succeed.

Self-assessment checklist for graphs:

Check point	Marks awarded	
	You	Your teacher
You have drawn the axes with a ruler, using most of the width and height of the grid.		
You have used a good scale for the x-axis and the y-axis, going up in 0.25 s, 0.5 s, 1 s or 2 s.		
You have labelled the axes correctly, giving the correct units for the scales on both axes.		
You have plotted each point precisely and correctly.		
You have used a small, neat cross or dot for each point.		
You have drawn a single, clear best-fit line through each set of points.		
You have ignored any anomalous results when drawing the line through each set of points.		
Total (out of 14)		

12–14   Excellent.
10–11   Good.
7–9   A good start, but you need to improve quite a bit.
5–6   Poor. Try this same graph again, using a new sheet of graph paper.
1–4   Very poor. Read through all the criteria again, and then try the same graph again.

Exercise C7.05 Finding the rate of a reaction producing a gas

> This exercise is based on an important practical technique of gas collection using a gas syringe. Following through the exercise should help develop your skills in presenting experimental data and calculating results from it. You will also be asked how the experiment could be modified to provide further data.

Hydrogen peroxide, H_2O_2, is an unstable compound that decomposes slowly at room temperature to form water and oxygen.

$$2H_2O_2(aq) \rightarrow 2H_2O(l) + O_2(g)$$

77

A student investigated how the rate of decomposition depends on the catalyst. She tested two catalysts: manganese(ɪv) oxide (Experiment **1**) and copper (Experiment **2**). The volume of oxygen produced by the reaction was measured at different times using the apparatus shown.

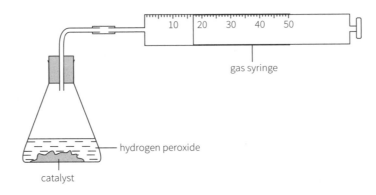

gas syringe

hydrogen peroxide

catalyst

a Use the data from the diagrams below to complete the results for Experiment **2** in Table 7.02.

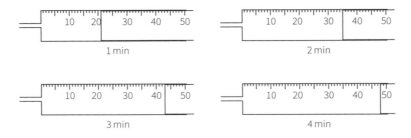

1 min

2 min

3 min

4 min

Time / min	1	2	3	4	5	6
Volume of oxygen collected in Experiment 1 / cm³	9	17	24	29	32	35
Volume of oxygen collected in Experiment 2 / cm³					50	50

Table 7.02

b Plot the results from Experiments **1** and **2** on the grid and draw a smooth curve through each set of points. Label the curves you draw as exp. **1** and exp. **2**.

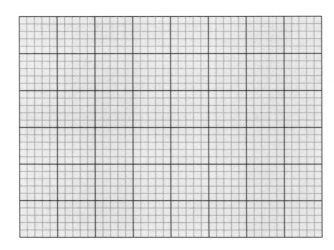

c Which of the two experiments was the first to reach completion? Explain your answer.

....

....

....

d Use your graph to estimate the time taken in Experiment **1** to double the volume of oxygen produced from 15 cm³ to 30 cm³. Record your answers in Table 7.03, and indicate on the graph how you obtained your values.

Time taken to produce 30 cm³ / min	
Time taken to produce 15 cm³ / min	
Time taken to double the volume from 15 cm³ to 30 cm³ / min	

Table 7.03 Experiment **1** (using manganese(IV) oxide)

e The rate (or speed) of a reaction may be calculated using the formula:

$$\text{rate of reaction} = \frac{\text{volume of oxygen produced / cm}^3}{\text{time taken / min}}$$

Using the two graphs and the above formula, calculate the rate of each reaction after the first 2.5 min for each experiment.

f From your answer to **e**, suggest which is the better catalyst, manganese(IV) oxide or copper. Explain your answer.

....

....

g At the end of Experiment **2** the copper was removed from the solution by filtration. It was dried and weighed. How would you predict this mass of copper would compare with the mass of copper added at the start of the experiment? Explain your answer.

....

....

h Suggest how the rate of decomposition in either experiment could be further increased.

....

....

....

Exercise C7.06 Runaway reactions

This exercise is designed to introduce the idea of 'runaway reactions' and to develop your data handling and interpretation skills.

A runaway reaction is a reaction which becomes uncontrollable. A common example is a reaction which is highly exothermic. During an exothermic reaction, the reaction mixture increases in temperature, and this further increases the rate of reaction. Heat is then produced more rapidly and the rate increases further. In an industrial process, this can cause an explosion and great danger to people living around the site.

A student carried out an investigation using the reaction between magnesium and sulfuric acid. He was investigating ways of controlling very exothermic reactions.

In each experiment, he took $10\ cm^3$ of sulfuric acid, noted its temperature and then added 0.1 g of magnesium ribbon. He measured the volume of gas produced in the first 30 s of the reaction and noted the temperature when the reaction stopped.

To make the reaction a fair test, he kept the amounts of magnesium and sulfuric acid the same in each experiment, but he changed the conditions by adding a different volume of water to the acid in each case before adding the magnesium.

The student's results are shown in Table 7.04.

Volume of water added / cm^3	Concentration of acid / mol/dm^3	Starting temperature / °C	Final temperature / °C	Temperature change / °C	Volume of gas collected in 30 s / cm^3
0	1.00	21	53	32	42
5		21	44		27
10		21	38		21
15		21	34		17
20		21	30		13
30		21	27		10
40	0.20	21	25	4	7

Table 7.04

a Complete Table 7.04 by filling in the second and fifth columns.

b Plot graphs of the data on the grid provided.

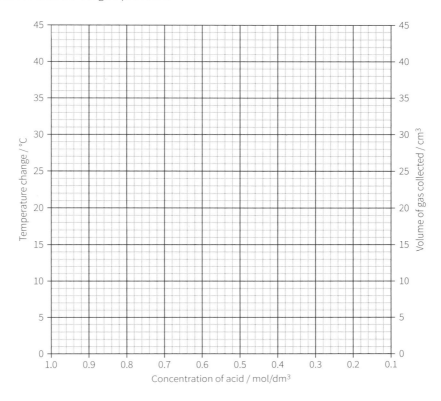

Temperature change / °C

Volume of gas collected / cm³

Concentration of acid / mol/dm³

c Unusually, the horizontal (*x*) axis has been shown with a decreasing scale of concentration values.

   i If concentration is decreasing, what property of the solution is increasing?

   ....

   ii What effect is plotting the graphs in this way designed to emphasise?

   ....

   ....

d Why can you be sure that the amount of energy produced in each reaction is the same?

....

e Why is the temperature change different in each case?

....

f What do the volumes of gas collected tell you about the rate of the different reactions?

....

....

g In industry, three things are important:

- safety (of the factory, the workers and the environment)
- how much product is made (the more the better)
- how quickly the product is produced (the more quickly the better).

Bearing this in mind, what advice would you give a factory that was going to use the reaction between magnesium and sulfuric acid on a large scale?

....

....

....

....

....

Use the checklist below to give yourself a mark for your graph. For each point, award yourself:
- **2 marks if you did it really well**
- **1 mark if you made a good attempt at it, and partly succeeded**
- **0 marks if you did not try to do it, or did not succeed.**

Self-assessment checklist for graphs:

Check point	Marks awarded	
	You	Your teacher
You have plotted each point precisely and correctly for both sets of data – using the different scales on the two horizontal axes.		
You have used a small, neat cross or dot for the points of one graph.		
You have used a small, but different, symbol for the points of the other graph.		
You have drawn a best-fit line through one set of points.		
You have drawn a best-fit line through the other set of points using a different colour or broken line.		
You have ignored any anomalous results when drawing the lines.		
Total (out of 12)		

10–12 Excellent.

7–9 Good.

4–6 A good start, but you need to improve quite a bit.

2–3 Poor. Try this same graph again, using a new sheet of graph paper.

1 Very poor. Read through all the criteria again, and then try the same graph again.

Chapter C8
Patterns and properties of metals

USEFUL REACTIONS AND THEIR EQUATIONS

$2Na + 2H_2O \longrightarrow 2NaOH + H_2$

$Fe_2O_3 + 2Al \longrightarrow Al_2O_3 + 2Fe$

$Zn(s) + CuSO_4(aq) \longrightarrow ZnSO_4(aq) + Cu(s)$

Exercise C8.01 Group I: The alkali metals

> This exercise should help you learn certain key properties of the alkali metals, and help develop the skills of predicting the properties of unfamiliar elements from the features of those that you have learnt.

Caesium is an alkali metal. It is in Group I of the Periodic Table.

a State **two** physical properties of caesium.

....

....

b State the number of electrons in the outer shell of a caesium atom ....

c Complete Table 8.01 to estimate the boiling point and atomic radius of caesium. Comment also on the reactivity of potassium and caesium with water.

Group I metal	Density / g/cm³	Radius of metal atom / nm	Boiling point / °C	Reactivity with water
sodium	0.97	0.191	883	floats and fizzes quickly on the surface, disappears gradually and does not burst into flame
potassium	0.86	0.235	760	
rubidium	1.53	0.250	686	reacts instantaneously, fizzes and bursts into flame, then spits violently and may explode
caesium	1.88			

Table 8.01

d Write the word equation for the reaction of caesium with water.

....

Exercise C8.02 The reactivity series of metals

This exercise should help you familiarise yourself with certain aspects of the reactivity series. It should also help develop your skills in interpreting practical observations and predicting the properties of unfamiliar elements from the features of those that you have learnt.

Using the results of various different types of chemical reaction, the metals can be arranged into the reactivity series.

a Magnesium reacts very slowly indeed with cold water but it does react strongly with steam to give magnesium oxide and a gas. Write the word equation for the reaction between magnesium and steam.

....

b Choose one metal from the reactivity series that will not react with steam.

....

c Choose one metal from the reactivity series that will safely react with dilute sulfuric acid.

....

d In each of the experiments below, a piece of metal is placed in a solution of a metal salt. Complete Table 8.02 of observations.

		zinc iron(II) sulfate solution	zinc copper(II) sulfate solution	iron copper(II) sulfate solution	silver copper(II) sulfate solution	copper silver nitrate solution
At start	**colour of metal**	grey		silver-coloured	silver-coloured	
	colour of solution	pale green		blue	blue	colourless
At finish	**colour of metal**	coated with metallic crystals		coated with brown solid	silver-coloured	coated with silver-coloured crystals
	colour of solution	colourless		pale green	blue	

Table 8.02

e Use these results to place the metals copper, iron, silver, zinc in order of reactivity (putting the most reactive metal first).

.... > .... > .... > ....

The reactivity series of metals given in Table 8.03 contains both familiar and unfamiliar elements. The unfamiliar elements are marked with an asterisk (*). Choose metal(s) from this list to answer the following questions.

f Which **two** metals would not react with dilute hydrochloric acid?

....

g Which **two** unfamiliar metals would react with cold water?

....

barium*
lanthanum*
aluminium
zinc
chromium*
iron
copper
palladium*

Table 8.03

h Name an unfamiliar metal that could not be extracted from its oxide by reduction with carbon.

....

Exercise C8.03 Energy from displacement reactions

This exercise will help you practise the presentation and interpretation of practical experiments.

When a metal is added to a solution of the salt of a less reactive metal, a displacement reaction takes place. The equations for two different examples are:

$$Fe(s) + CuSO_4(aq) \rightarrow Cu(s) + FeSO_4(aq)$$

$$zinc + copper\ sulfate \rightarrow copper + zinc\ sulfate$$

The energy change involved in these reactions can be measured by adding 5 g of metal powder to 50 cm³ of 0.5 mol/dm³ copper(II) sulfate solution in a polystyrene cup. The temperature of the solution is taken before adding the metal. The powder is then added, the reaction mixture is stirred continuously, and temperatures are taken every 30 s for 3 min.

A student took the readings that follow when carrying out this experiment.

Time / min	0.0	0.5	1.0	1.5	2.0	2.5	3.0
Experiment 1 (zinc): temperature / °C	21	48	62	71	75	72	70
Experiment 2 (iron): temperature / °C	21	25	32	38	41	43	44

Table 8.03

a Plot **two** graphs on the grid provided and label each with the name of the metal.

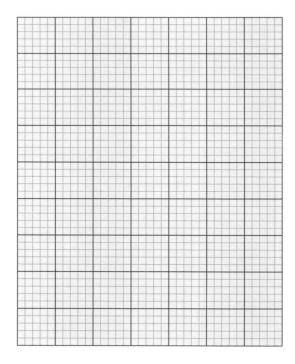

b Write the word equation for the first reaction and the balanced symbol equation for the second.

....

....

c Which metal, iron or zinc, produced the larger temperature rise?

....

d Suggest why this metal gave the larger temperature rise.

....

....

e Comment on whether this experiment is a 'fair test'. Explain your answer.

....

....

Use the checklist below to give yourself a mark for your graph. For each point, award yourself:

- **2 marks if you did it really well**
- **1 mark if you made a good attempt at it, and partly succeeded**
- **0 marks if you did not try to do it, or did not succeed.**

Self-assessment checklist for graphs:

Check point	Marks awarded	
	You	Your teacher
You have drawn the axes with a ruler, using most of the width and height of the grid.		
You have used a good scale for the x-axis and the y-axis, going up in useful proportions.		
You have labelled the axes correctly giving the correct units for the scales on both axes.		
You have plotted each point precisely and correctly.		
You have used a small, neat dot or cross for each point.		
You have drawn a single, clear best-fit line through each set of points – using a ruler for a straight line.		
You have ignored any anomalous results when drawing the lines through each set of results.		
Total (out of 14)		

12–14 Excellent.

10–11 Good.

7–9 A good start, but you need to improve quite a bit.

5–6 Poor. Try this same graph again, using a new sheet of graph paper.

1–4 Very poor. Read through all the criteria again, and then try the same graph again.

Exercise C8.04 Metals and alloys

This exercise discusses some aspects of alloys and their usefulness. It explores the advantages and specific purpose of certain alloys.

Table 8.04 shows some properties of a selection of pure metals.

Metal	Relative abundance in Earth's crust	Cost of extraction	Density	Strength	Melting point / °C	Electrical conductivity relative to iron
iron	2nd	low	high	high	1535	1.0
titanium	7th	very high	low	high	1660	0.2
aluminium	1st	high	low	medium	660	3.5
zinc	19th	low	high	low	419	1.7
copper	20th	low	high	medium	1083	6.0
tin	40th	low	high	low	231	0.9
lead	30th	low	very high	low	327	0.5

Table 8.04

Use information from Table 8.04 to answer the following questions.

a Why is aluminium used for overhead power cables?

....

b Why do the aluminium cables have an iron (or steel) core?

....

c Why is copper used instead of aluminium in wiring in the home?

....

d Why is titanium a good metal to use for jet aircraft and Formula 1 racing cars?

....

....

Alloys have different properties from the metals they are made from. They are usually harder and stronger with lower melting points.

e **Solder**, which is melted to join together electrical components on circuit boards is a mixture of tin and lead. Suggest why it is used in preference to the pure metals.

....

....

f **Brass** is an alloy of copper and zinc. It is used to make brass musical instruments and to make electrical connectors and plugs.

There are two main types of brass: 60 : 40 and 70 : 30 copper to zinc. The larger the amount of zinc, the harder and stronger the alloy is.

Suggest which alloy is used for each of the purposes mentioned above. Give a reason for your answers.

Cu60 : Zn40

....

....

Cu70 : Zn30

....

....

Chapter C9
Industrial inorganic chemistry

USEFUL REACTIONS AND THEIR EQUATIONS

$Fe_2O_3 + 3CO \longrightarrow 2Fe + 3CO_2$	blast furnace reaction
$CaCO_3 \longrightarrow CaO + CO_2$	lime kiln reaction
$Al^{3+}(l) + 3e^- \longrightarrow Al(l)$	extraction of aluminium
$N_2(g) + 3H_2(g) \rightleftharpoons 2NH_3(g)$	Haber process
$2SO_2(g) + O_2(g) \rightleftharpoons 2SO_3(g)$	Contact process

Exercise C9.01 Metal alloys and their uses

This exercise should help you recall details of different alloys and the basis of their usefulness.

Complete Table 9.01 about the composition and usefulness of some alloys by filling in the gaps.

Alloy	Composition	Use	Useful property
mild steel	iron: >99.75% carbon: <0.25%	....	....
stainless steel	iron: 74% ....: 18% nickel: 8%	........................, surgical instruments, chemical vessels for industry	....
brass	copper: 70% ....: 30%	.... instruments, ornaments	'gold' colour, harder than copper
bronze	copper: 95% ....: 5%	statues, church bells	hard, does not ....
aerospace aluminium	aluminium: 90.25% zinc: 6% magnesium: 2.5% copper: 1.25%	aircraft construction	....
solder	tin: 60% lead: 40%	....	low melting point
tungsten steel	iron: 95% tungsten: 5%	cutting edges of drill bits	....

Table 9.01

Exercise C9.02 Extracting aluminium by electrolysis

> This exercise should help you recall and understand the details of the method for extracting aluminium.

Because of its high reactivity, aluminium must be extracted by electrolysis. The electrolyte is aluminium oxide dissolved in molten cryolite. Hydrated aluminium oxide is heated to produce the pure aluminium oxide used.

$$Al_2O_3 \cdot 3H_2O \qquad \rightarrow \qquad Al_2O_3 + 3H_2O$$
hydrated aluminium oxide

a What type of reaction is this? Put a ring around the correct answer.

decomposition   neutralisation   oxidation   reduction

b Why must the electrolyte be molten for electrolysis to occur?

....

c What is the purpose of the cryolite?

....

d The following diagram shows an electrolysis cell. Which letter (**A**, **B**, **C** or **D**) represents the cathode?

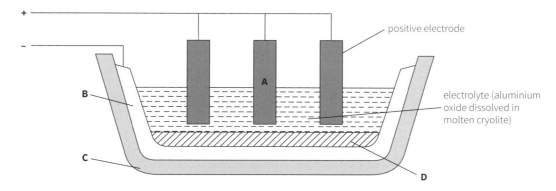

e State the name of the products formed at the anode and cathode during this electrolysis.

At the anode: ....   At the cathode: ....

f Why do the anodes have to be renewed periodically?

....

g Complete the equation for the formation of aluminium from aluminium ions.

$$Al^{3+} + ...e^- \rightarrow Al$$

h State **one** use of aluminium.

....

Exercise C9.03 The importance of nitrogen

The following exercise connects the ideas surrounding the importance of nitrogen to agriculture and develops your understanding of chemical equilibria. It also develops your skills in processing and interpreting experimental results.

Although certain bacteria in the soil convert nitrogen gas into nitrates, other bacteria convert nitrogen into ammonium salts. The ionic equation for this second reaction is:

$$N_2 + 8H^+ + 6e^- \rightarrow 2NH_4^+$$

a Explain why this is a reduction reaction.

....

b In the presence of hydrogen ions, bacteria of a different type convert nitrate ions into nitrogen gas and water. Give the ionic equation for this reaction.

....

Ammonia is made by the Haber process using an iron catalyst.

$$N_2 + 3H_2 \rightleftharpoons 2NH_3 \quad \text{(the forward reaction is exothermic)}$$

The raw materials for the Haber process can be obtained from the air and from natural gas.

c What method is used to separate pure nitrogen from other gases in the air?

....

d Describe how hydrogen can be made from hydrocarbons.

....

....

e State the essential conditions of temperature and pressure used for the Haber process.

....

f Sketch an energy profile diagram to show both the catalysed and the uncatalysed reaction. Label the diagram to show the following key features: the reactants and products, the enthalpy change for the reaction, and the catalysed and uncatalysed reactions.

Table 9.02 shows how the percentage of ammonia in the mixture leaving the reaction vessel varies under different conditions.

Pressure / atm	100	200	300	400
% of ammonia at 300 °C	45	65	72	78
% of ammonia at 500 °C	9	18	25	31

Table 9.02

g Use the grid provided to plot graphs of the percentage of ammonia against pressure at both 300 °C and 500 °C.

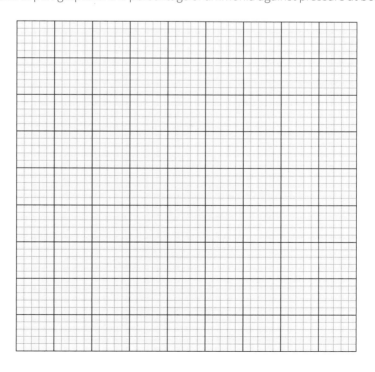

Use the checklist below to give yourself a mark for your graph. For each point, award yourself:

- 2 marks if you did it really well
- 1 mark if you made a good attempt at it, and partly succeeded
- 0 marks if you did not try to do it, or did not succeed.

Self-assessment checklist for graphs:

Check point	Marks awarded	
	You	Your teacher
You have drawn the axes with a ruler, using most of the width and height of the grid.		
You have used a good scale for the x-axis and the y-axis, going up in useful proportions.		
You have labelled the axes correctly, giving the correct units for the scales on both axes.		
You have plotted each point precisely and correctly.		
You have used a small, neat dot or cross for each point.		
You have drawn a single, clear best-fit line through each set of points – using a ruler for any straight line.		
You have ignored any anomalous results when drawing the line.		
Total (out of 14)		

12–14	Excellent.
10–11	Good.
7–9	A good start, but you need to improve quite a bit.
5–6	Poor. Try this same graph again, using a new sheet of graph paper.
1–4	Very poor. Read through all the criteria again, and then try the same graph again.

h   What is the percentage of ammonia formed at 250 atm and 300 °C?

   ....

i   Use your graphs to estimate the percentage of ammonia formed at 400 °C and 250 atm.

   ....

j   The advantage of using a low temperature is the large percentage of ammonia formed. What is the disadvantage of using a low temperature?

   ....

k   Suggest **two** advantages of using high pressure in the manufacture of ammonia.

   ....

   ....

The most important use of ammonia is in fertiliser production. Fertilisers are added to the soil to improve crop yields. A farmer has the choice of two fertilisers, ammonium nitrate, NH_4NO_3, or diammonium hydrogen phosphate, $(NH_4)_2HPO_4$.

l   Show by calculation which of these fertilisers contains the greater percentage of nitrogen by mass.

m   State **one** major problem caused when the nitrates from fertilisers leach from the soil into streams and rivers.

....

Exercise C9.04   Making sulfuric acid industrially

> **This exercise helps your understanding of chemical equilibria, particularly the factors involved in the Contact process.**

The diagram shows the three different stages in the manufacture of sulfuric acid.

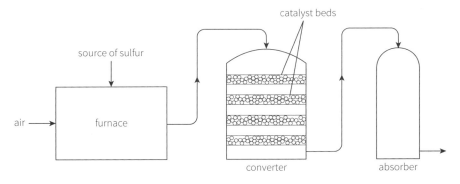

One possible source of sulfur is an ore containing zinc sulfide, ZnS. In the furnace, this sulfide ore is heated in oxygen to make zinc oxide, ZnO, and sulfur dioxide.

a   Write an equation for this reaction.

....

In the converter, sulfur dioxide and oxygen are passed over a series of catalyst beds at a temperature of about 420 °C.

$$2SO_2(g) + O_2(g) \rightleftharpoons 2SO_3(g) \qquad \Delta H = -196 \text{ kJ (the reaction is exothermic)}$$

b   An increase in pressure increases the yield of sulfur trioxide. Explain the reason for this effect.

....

....

c   Even though an increase in pressure increases the yield of sulfur trioxide, the reaction in the converter is carried out at atmospheric pressure. Suggest a reason for this.

....

....

95

d In some sulfuric acid plants, the gases are cooled when they pass from one catalyst bed to the next. Use the information given about the nature of the reaction to explain why the gases need to be cooled.

....

....

Exercise C9.05 Concrete chemistry

This exercise will aid your recall of the important uses of limestone and help your familiarity with questions asked in an unusual context.

Limestone is an important mineral resource. One use is in the making of cement. Cement is made by heating clay with crushed limestone. During this process (illustrated in diagram below), the calcium carbonate is first converted to calcium oxide.

$$CaCO_3 \rightarrow CaO + CO_2$$

a What name is given to this type of chemical reaction?

....

Concrete is then made from cement, sand and water. When it has set, concrete is slightly porous. Rainwater can soak into concrete and some of the unreacted calcium oxide present dissolves to form calcium hydroxide.

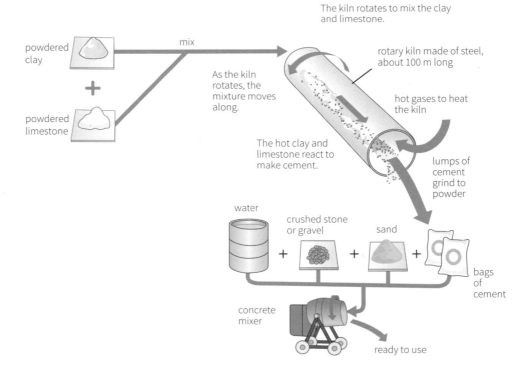

b Write an equation for the reaction that produces calcium hydroxide.

....

The aqueous calcium hydroxide in wet concrete is able to react with carbon dioxide in the air.

$$Ca(OH)_2 + CO_2 \rightarrow CaCO_3 + H_2O$$

The diagram shows how the pH can vary at different points inside a cracked concrete beam.

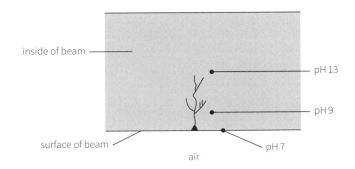

c Describe the change in pH from the surface to the centre of the beam, and explain why this variation occurs.

....

....

....

....

d Describe briefly **two** other uses for limestone in addition to making cement.

....

....

....

....

Exercise C9.06 The chlor–alkali industry

This exercise is concerned with the industrial electrolysis of brine and emphasises the usefulness and wide range of the products formed by this process (see diagram below).

The electrolysis of brine is arguably one of the most efficient industrial processes. This stems from the fact that all of the major products act as the starting points for the manufacture of other useful chemicals. There is essentially no waste product from the process.

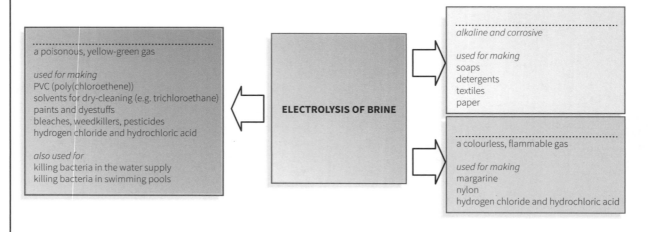

....
a poisonous, yellow-green gas

used for making
PVC (poly(chloroethene))
solvents for dry-cleaning (e.g. trichloroethane)
paints and dyestuffs
bleaches, weedkillers, pesticides
hydrogen chloride and hydrochloric acid

also used for
killing bacteria in the water supply
killing bacteria in swimming pools

ELECTROLYSIS OF BRINE

....
alkaline and corrosive

used for making
soaps
detergents
textiles
paper

....
a colourless, flammable gas

used for making
margarine
nylon
hydrogen chloride and hydrochloric acid

a The starting point for this industrial process is a concentrated brine solution (the term 'brine' is explained in the coursebook).

i What is **brine**?

....

ii What are the **three** major products of the electrolysis of brine? List them below and write their names in on the diagram above.

....

b Two of the products of the electrolysis can be reacted together to produce sodium chlorate(ı) and sodium chlorate(v). These are commercial products that are sold as bleach and weedkiller respectively.

i Complete the following word equation for the production of sodium chlorate(ı).

.... + ... $\rightarrow$ sodium + sodium + water
....   chlorate(ı)   chloride

ii Sodium chlorate(ı) is used as a bleach but also as a treatment for the domestic water supply and swimming pools. What is the purpose of this treatment?

....

iii Sodium chlorate(v) is an ionic compound made up of sodium ions and chlorate(v) ions (ClO_3^-). What is the formula of sodium chlorate(v)?

....

iv   The two gases produced in the electrolysis of brine can be reacted together to form hydrogen chloride. Write the word and balanced symbol equations for this reaction.

....

....

c   The membrane cell for the electrolysis of brine is shown in the following diagram.

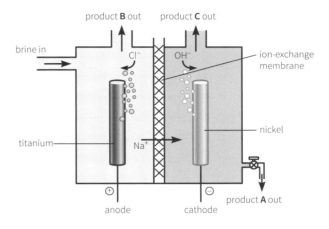

i   What is the purpose of the membrane in the electrolysis cell?

....

....

ii   Why is the anode made of titanium?

....

iii   Write the half-equations for the reactions taking place at the anode and cathode. Include state symbols in your equations.

At the anode: ....

At the cathode: ....

d   Chlorine is reacted with various hydrocarbons to produce useful solvents. For example, chlorine reacts with ethene to produce 1,2-dichloroethane.

i   What type of reaction is this?

....

ii   What is the structural formula of 1,2-dichloroethane?

Chapter C10
Organic chemistry

KEY TERMS

hydrocarbon: a compound that contains carbon and hydrogen only

saturated hydrocarbon: a hydrocarbon that contains only single covalent bonds between the carbon atoms

alkane: a saturated hydrocarbon that contains only single covalent bonds between the carbon atoms of the chain; the simplest alkane is methane, CH_4

alkene: an unsaturated hydrocarbon that contains at least one double bond between two of the carbon atoms in the chain; the simplest alkene is ethene, C_2H_4

homologous series: a family of organic compounds with similar chemical properties as they contain the same functional group; alkenes, alcohols, for instance

addition reaction: a reaction in which atoms, or groups, are added across a carbon-carbon double bond in an unsaturated molecule such as an alkene

USEFUL REACTIONS AND THEIR EQUATIONS

methane + oxygen $\longrightarrow$ carbon dioxide + water

CH_4 + $2O_2$ $\longrightarrow$ CO_2 + $2H_2O$ burning methane

ethanol + oxygen $\longrightarrow$ carbon dioxide + water

C_2H_5OH + $3O_2$ $\longrightarrow$ $2CO_2$ + $3H_2O$ burning ethanol

glucose $\longrightarrow$ ethanol + carbon dioxide

$C_6H_{12}O_6$ $\longrightarrow$ $2C_2H_5OH$ + $2CO_2$ fermentation

Exercise C10.01 Families of hydrocarbons

This exercise helps you revise the key features of the families of hydrocarbons and develops your understanding of the structures of organic compounds.

a Complete the passage using only words from the list.

bromine	alkanes	hydrogen	double	chlorine	chains	petroleum
methane	ethene	ethane	colourless	propane	alkenes	

The chief source of organic compounds is the naturally occurring mixture of hydrocarbons known

as .... Hydrocarbons are compounds that contain carbon and .... only.

There are many hydrocarbons because of the ability of carbon atoms to join together to form

long .... There is a series of hydrocarbons with just single covalent bonds between

the carbon atoms in the molecule. These are saturated hydrocarbons, and they are called ....

The simplest of these saturated hydrocarbons has the formula CH_4 and is called .... Unsaturated

hydrocarbons can also occur. These molecules contain at least one carbon–carbon .... bond.

These compounds belong to the .... a second series of hydrocarbons. The simplest of this 'family' of unsaturated hydrocarbons has the formula C_2H_4 and is known as ....

The test for an unsaturated hydrocarbon is to add the sample to .... water. It changes colour from orange/brown to .... if the hydrocarbon is unsaturated.

b Table 10.01 shows the names, formulae and boiling points of the first members of the homologous series of unsaturated hydrocarbons. Complete the table by filling in the spaces.

Name	Formula	Boiling point / °C
	C_2H_4	−102
propene	C_3H_6	−48
butene	C_4H_8	−7
pentene	C_5H_{10}	30
hexene		

Table 10.01

c Deduce the molecular formula of the alkene which has a relative molecular mass of 168.

....

Exercise C10.02 Unsaturated hydrocarbons (the alkenes)

> **This exercise develops your understanding of unsaturated hydrocarbons using an unfamiliar example.**

Limonene is a colourless unsaturated hydrocarbon found in oranges and lemons. The structure of limonene is shown in the diagram.

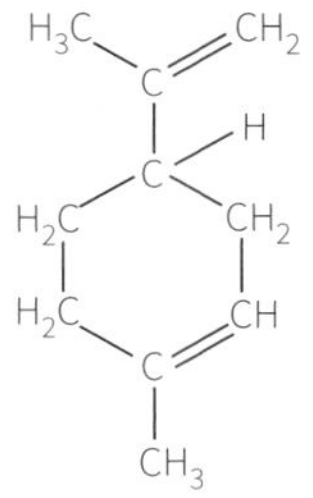

a On the structure, draw a circle around the bonds which make limonene an unsaturated hydrocarbon.

b What is the molecular formula of limonene?

....

c Describe the colour change which occurs when excess limonene is added to a few drops of bromine water.

....

The diagram shows how limonene can be extracted from lemon peel by steam distillation.

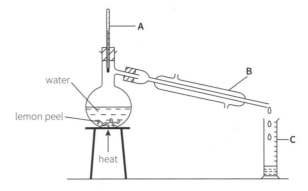

d State the name of the pieces of apparatus labelled **A**, **B** and **C**.

A .... B .... C ....

When limonene undergoes incomplete combustion, carbon monoxide is formed.

e What do you understand by the term 'incomplete combustion'?

....

....

f State an adverse effect of carbon monoxide on health.

....

....

g All hydrocarbons are covalently bonded whether saturated or unsaturated. Draw 'dot-and-cross' diagrams for methane and ethane illustrating the arrangement of the bonding electrons. You only need to draw the outer electrons of the carbon atoms.

Exercise C10.03 The alcohols as fuels

The following exercise uses information relating to the alcohols to develop your understanding of these compounds and to enhance your presentation, analysis and interpretation of experimental data concerning their property as fuels.

Table 10.02 shows the formulae of the first three members of the alcohol homologous series.

Alcohol	Formula
methanol	CH_3OH
ethanol	C_2H_5OH
propanol	C_3H_7OH

Table 10.02

a Use the information given to deduce the general formula for the alcohol homologous series.

....

Ethanol, the most significant of the alcohols, can be manufactured from either ethene or glucose.

b Write an equation for the industrial production of ethanol from ethene and state the conditions under which the reaction takes place.

....

....

The fermentation (anaerobic respiration) of glucose by yeast can be represented by the following equation. The reaction is catalysed by the enzyme zymase. After a few days, the reaction stops. It has produced a 12% aqueous solution of ethanol.

$$C_6H_{12}O_6 \longrightarrow 2C_2H_5OH + 2CO_2$$

c Sketch a labelled diagram to show how fermentation can be carried out.

d Suggest a reason why the reaction stops after a few days.

....

....

e Why is it essential that there is no oxygen in the reaction vessel?

....

....

f Name the products of the complete combustion of ethanol.

....

g Explain why ethanol made from ethene is a non-renewable fuel, but that made from glucose is a renewable fuel.

....

....

....

A student used the apparatus shown in the diagram below to investigate the amount of heat produced when ethanol was burnt.

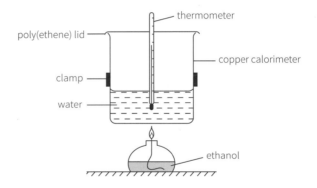

h Draw the structure of ethanol showing all atoms and bonds.

i Complete the equation for the complete combustion of ethanol.

$$C_2H_5OH + 3O_2 \rightarrow \text{................} CO_2 + \text{................} H_2O$$

j When 2.3 g of ethanol are burnt, 2.7 g of water are formed. Calculate the mass of water formed when 13.8 g of ethanol are burnt.

The experiment was later adapted to compare the heat released by burning four different alcohols. Each burner in turn was weighed and then the alcohol was allowed to burn until the temperature of the water had risen by 15 °C. The flame was then extinguished and the burner re-weighed. The results obtained are shown in Table 10.03.

Alcohol	Formula	Mass of alcohol burnt / g
methanol	CH_3OH	0.90
ethanol	C_2H_5OH	0.70
propan-1-ol	C_3H_7OH	0.62
pentan-1-ol	$C_5H_{11}OH$	0.57

Table 10.03

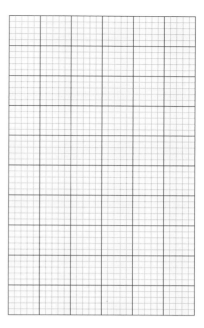

k Plot a graph showing how the mass of alcohol required varies with the number of carbon atoms in the alcohol used. Draw a smooth curve through the points.

Use the checklist below to give yourself a mark for your graph. For each point, award yourself:

- **2 marks if you did it really well**
- **1 mark if you made a good attempt at it, and partly succeeded**
- **0 marks if you did not try to do it, or did not succeed.**

Self-assessment checklist for graphs:

Check point	Marks awarded	
	You	Your teacher
You have drawn the axes with a ruler, using most of the width and height of the grid.		
You have used a good scale for the x-axis and the y-axis, going up in useful proportions.		
You have labelled the axes correctly, giving the correct units for the scales on both axes.		
You have plotted each point precisely and correctly.		
You have used a small, neat cross or dot for each point.		
You have drawn a single, clear best-fit line through the points.		
You have ignored any anomalous results when drawing the line.		
Total (out of 14)		

12–14 Excellent.

10–11 Good.

7–9 A good start, but you need to improve quite a bit.

5–6 Poor. Try this same graph again, using a new sheet of graph paper.

1–4 Very poor. Read through all the criteria again, and then try the same graph again.

l   Predict the mass of butanol, C_4H_9OH, which, on combustion, would raise the temperature of the water by 15 °C.

....

m   Suggest a reason why the same temperature rise (15 °C) was used in each experiment.

....

....

Exercise C10.04 Hydrocarbons and their reactions

This exercise is aimed at developing your confidence in discussing aspects of the chemistry of the hydrocarbons, particularly their use as fuels.

a   Complete Table 10.04. (Relative atomic masses: H = 1, C = 12.)

Name of hydrocarbon	ethane	ethene
Molecular formula of hydrocarbon	C_2H_6	
Relative molecular mass of hydrocarbon		
Structural formula of hydrocarbon		
Colour of bromine water after being shaken with the hydrocarbon		colourless

Table 10.04

b   The hydrocarbon propane is an important constituent of the fuel liquid petroleum gas (LPG). For the burning of propane in an excess of air, give:

i   a word equation

....

ii   a balanced symbol equation.

....

iii   Use your answer to give the number of moles of water formed when one mole of propane is burnt in an excess of air.

....

c Unsaturated hydrocarbons take part in addition reactions.

    i Write a word equation for the reaction between propene and hydrogen.

    ....

    ii Write a symbol equation for the reaction between butene and steam.

    ....

d A major use of LPG is in various forms of bottled gas. This gas which can be used for barbecues and domestic and patio heaters involves using propane and/or butane under pressure in canisters.

    i Carry out an internet search to find out which of these gases gives the most heat for a given mass of gas.

    ....

    ....

    ....

    ....

    ii For bottled mixtures of LPG, the proportions of propane and butane in the mixture are changed seasonally. One gas is preferred in the winter, the other in summer. Research the nature of this preference and why it is made.

    ....

    ....

    ....

    ....

Chapter C11
Petrochemicals and polymers

KEY TERMS

fossil fuel: a fuel formed underground from previously living material by the action of heat and pressure over geological periods of time

cracking: a thermal decomposition reaction in which a long-chain saturated alkane is broken down to a shorter alkane, usually with the formation of an alkene

catalytic cracking: cracking carried out in the presence of a catalyst

monomer: the small molecules from which polymers are built by joining them together

polymer: a long-chain molecule made by joining many monomer molecules together

polymerisation: the process by which a long-chain polymer is made from its monomers

addition polymerisation: a polymerisation process in which the monomers contain a carbon–carbon double bond and polymerisation takes place by addition reactions

condensation polymerisation: a polymerisation process in which the linking of the monomers takes place by a condensation reaction in which a small molecule, usually water, is eliminated

USEFUL EQUATIONS AND THEIR STRUCTURES

$$C_{10}H_{22} \rightarrow C_8H_{18} + C_2H_4 \qquad \text{cracking}$$

$$n C_2H_4 \rightarrow -(C_2H_4)_n-$$
$$n CH_2CHCl \rightarrow -(CH_2CHCl)_n- \qquad \Big\} \quad \text{addition polymerisation}$$

The following diagrams represent the structures of the addition polymer, poly(ethene) and the condensation polymers nylon, a protein, a polyester (terylene) and a polysaccharide (starch), respectively. Remember you need only show how the linkage is formed in each case. Water is usually the other product of the reaction.

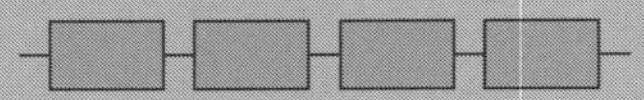

poly(ethene)

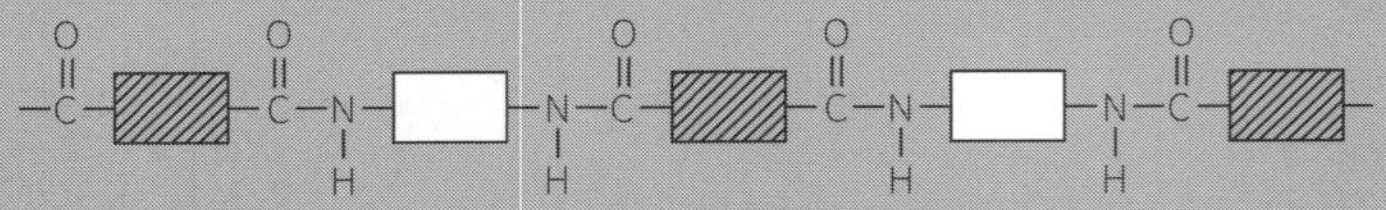

nylon

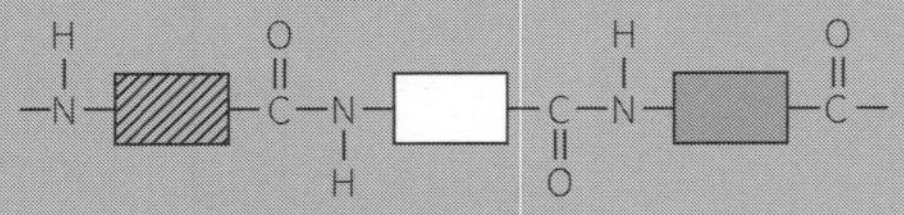

protein

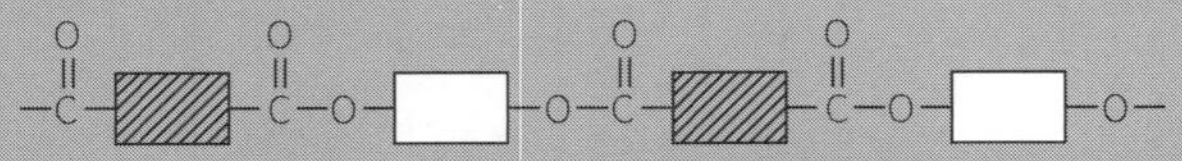

terylene

starch

Exercise C11.01 Essential processes of the petrochemical industry

> This exercise aids you in recalling and understanding two of the main processes of the petrochemical industry.

Petroleum (crude oil) is a raw material which is processed in an oil refinery. Two of the processes used are **fractional distillation** and **cracking**.

a The diagram shows the fractional distillation of petroleum. Give the name and a major use for each fraction.

A ....

B ....

C ....

D ....

E ....

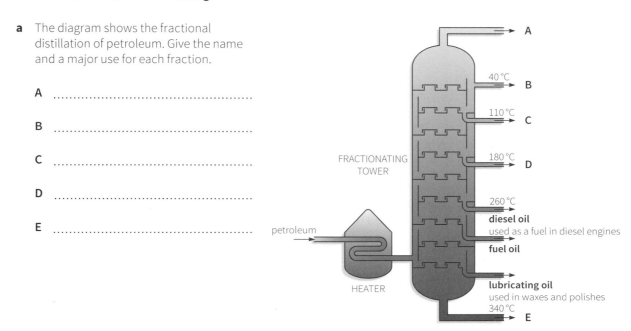

Table 11.01 shows the percentage by mass of some of these different fractions in petroleum. Also shown is the demand for each fraction expressed as a percentage.

Fraction	Number of carbon atoms per molecule	Percentage in petroleum / %	Percentage needed by the oil refinery to supply demand / %
A	1–4	4	11
B	5–9	11	22
C	10–14	12	20
D	14–20	18	15
waxes and E	over 20	23	4

Table 11.01

b Which physical property is used to separate petroleum by fractional distillation?

....

c Define the term 'cracking'.

....

....

109

d Use information from the table to explain how cracking helps an oil refinery match the supply of gasoline (petrol) with the demand for gasoline.

....

....

....

e The hydrocarbon $C_{15}H_{32}$ can be cracked to make propene and one other hydrocarbon.

    i Write an equation for this reaction.

       ....

    ii Draw the structure of propene.

Exercise C11.02 Addition polymerisation

> **This exercise will help you practise the representation of polymers and develop your understanding of their uses and the issues involved.**

a Poly(ethene) is a major plastic used for making a wide variety of containers. Complete these sentences about poly(ethene) using words from this list.

acids	addition	condensation	ethane
polymerisation	ethene	monomers	polymer

Poly(ethene) is a .... formed by the .... of .... molecules. In this reaction, the

starting molecules can be described as ....; the process is known as ....

b Draw the structure of poly(ethene) showing **at least two** repeat units.

The diagram below shows the structure of an addition polymer, **X**.

c Draw the structure of the monomer from which polymer **X** is formed.

d Polymer **X** is non-biodegradable. Describe one pollution problem that this causes.

....

....

e Polymer **X** can be disposed of by burning at high temperature. However, this can produce toxic waste gases such as hydrogen chloride. Hydrogen chloride can be removed from the waste gases by reaction with moist calcium carbonate powder. Name the three products of this reaction.

....

Exercise C11.03 Representing condensation polymerisation reactions

> **This exercise is designed to develop your confidence in understanding and drawing the schematic representations of the different condensation polymerisation reactions.**

Condensation polymerisation is important in the formation of both natural and synthetic macromolecules. The monomers involved are bifunctional. They have functional groups at both ends of the molecule.

There are various types of important condensation polymers. In each case, the reaction to form the polymer can be represented by a schematic diagram which shows only the key interactions between the functional groups and the nature of the linkage involved.

a Two monomers are represented below.

i Name the type of polymer formed using this combination of monomers.

ii Draw the structure of the polymer formed. Show **at least three** monomers joined together.

iii Name the synthetic polymer formed in this way.

....

b A form of the same polymer can be made from the two monomers are represented below (see Activity C11.05 in the coursebook).

Deduce the simple molecule released in the condensation reaction in this case.

....

Exercise C11.04 Meeting fuel demand

> This exercise is concerned with aspects of the use of petroleum fractions as fuels and how chemistry can be used to convert unwanted fractions into commercially useful resources.

Table 11.02 gives information on the proportions of certain fractions in a sample of petroleum from a particular oil-producing region. It also shows the commercial demand for these fractions.

Fraction	Proportion of this fraction in petroleum / %	Percentage demand / %
refinery gas	2	5
gasoline (petrol)	21	28
diesel oil	17	25
fuel oil and bitumen	47	34

Table 11.02

a Plot bar charts of the two sets of figures provided in Table 11.02 to compare the availability and demand of these fractions.

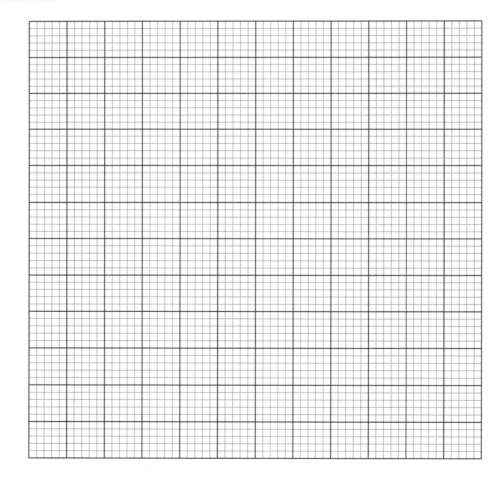

b The differences between these two sets of figures highlight the need for manipulation of the chemistry of the fractions.

i Which fractions are in greatest demand generally?

....

ii Which of the fractions has the lowest demand and is present in the smallest quantities in the petroleum? What is the relative size of the molecules in this fraction?

....

iii What is the total proportion of the demand that is used for fuelling cars and lorries?

....

iv What chemical process provides the answer to this imbalance between availability and demand?

....

c When the liquid alkane **decane** is cracked, a gas is formed which turns bromine water colourless.

i What does this test tell you about this gas?

....

ii What type of reaction takes place in this gas test?

....

The diagram shows part of the apparatus for cracking decane in the lab.

iii

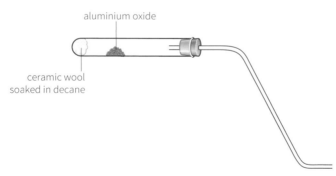

aluminium oxide

ceramic wool
soaked in decane

Complete the diagram to show how the gas is collected. Include a Bunsen valve in your diagram.

iv What is the aluminium oxide there for?

....

v Mark on the diagram an arrow where the test tube should be heated.

vi The moment heating is stopped, the delivery tube is removed from the gas-collecting system. Why is this done?

....

vii Complete this equation for the cracking of decane, and name the gas that is formed:

$$C_{10}H_{22} \rightarrow C_8H_{18} + ...$$

decane   octane   ....

Chapter C12
Chemical analysis and investigation

KEY TERMS

titration: a method of finding the amount of a substance in a solution

precipitation: the sudden appearance of a solid produced in a chemical reaction

ionic equation: an equation showing only those ions that participate in a reaction and the product of that reaction

USEFUL REACTIONS AND THEIR EQUATIONS

$AgNO_3(aq) + NaCl(aq) \longrightarrow AgCl(s) + NaNO_3(aq)$ or $Ag^+(aq) + Cl^-(aq) \longrightarrow AgCl(s)$

$Ba(NO_3)(aq) + CuSO_4(aq) \longrightarrow BaSO_4(s) + Cu(NO_3)_2(aq)$ or $Ba^{2+}(aq) + SO_4^{2-}(aq) \longrightarrow BaSO_4(s)$

$FeSO_4(aq) + 2NaOH(aq) \longrightarrow Fe(OH)_2(s) + Na_2SO_4(aq)$ or $Fe^{2+}(aq) + 2OH^-(aq) \longrightarrow Fe(OH)_2(s)$

Exercise C12.01 Chemical analysis

> This exercise will help familiarise you with some of the analytical tests and the strategy behind them. Remember that these tests can come up frequently on the written papers as well as on the practical papers.

a Table 12.01 shows the tests that some students did on substance **A** and the conclusions they made from their observations.

   i Complete the table by describing these observations and suggest the test and observation which led to the conclusion in test **4**.

Test	Observation	Conclusion
1 Solid **A** was dissolved in water and the solution divided into three parts for tests **2**, **3** and **4**.		**A** does not contain a transition metal.
2 i To the first part, aqueous sodium hydroxide was added until a change was seen.		**A** may contain Zn^{2+} ions or Al^{3+} ions.
ii Excess aqueous sodium hydroxide was added to the mixture from **i**.		
3 i To the second part aqueous ammonia was added until a change was seen.		The presence of Zn^{2+} ions is confirmed in **A**.
ii An excess of aqueous ammonia was added to the mixture from **i**.		

(Continued)

Test	Observation	Conclusion
4		**A** contains I⁻ ions.

Table 12.01

ii Give the name and formula of compound **A**.

....

b A mixture of powdered crystals contains both ammonium ions (NH_4^+) and zinc ions (Zn^{2+}). The two salts contain the same anion (negative ion).

The table below shows the results of tests carried out by a student.

i Complete Table 12.02 of observations made by the student.

Test	Observations
1 A sample of the solid mixture was dissolved in distilled water. The solution was acidified with dilute $HNO_3(aq)$ and a solution of $Ba(NO_3)$ added.	A white precipitate was formed.
2 A sample of the solid was placed in a test tube. NaOH(aq) was added and the mixture warmed. A piece of moist red litmus paper was held at the mouth of the tube.	The solid dissolved and pungent fumes were given off. The litmus paper turned ...., indicating the presence of .... ions.
3 A sample of the solid was dissolved in distilled water to give a .... solution. NaOH(aq) was added dropwise until in excess.	A .... precipitate was formed which was .... in excess alkali.
4 A further sample of the solid was dissolved in distilled water. Concentrated ammonia solution ($NH_3(aq)$) was added dropwise until in excess.	A .... precipitate was formed. On addition of excess alkali, the precipitate was ....

Table 12.02

ii Give the names and formulae of the two salts in the mixture.

....

iii Give the name and formula of the precipitate formed in tests **3** and **4**.

....

c   A mixture of two solids, **P** and **Q**, was analysed.

Solid **P** was the water-soluble salt aluminium sulfate, $Al_2(SO_4)_3$, and solid **Q** was an insoluble salt. The tests on the mixture and some of the observations are reported in the following table.

i   Complete the observations in Table 12.03.

Tests	Observations
Distilled water was added to the mixture of **P** and **Q** in a boiling tube. The boiling tube was shaken and the contents of the tube then filtered, keeping the filtrate and residue for the following tests. The filtrate was divided into five test tubes in order to carry out tests **1** to **5**.	
Tests on the filtrate **1** Appearance of the first sample of the filtrate.	
2 Drops of aqueous sodium hydroxide were added to the second portion of the solution and the test tube shaken. Excess aqueous sodium hydroxide was then added to the test tube.	
3 Aqueous ammonia was added to the third portion, dropwise and then in excess.	

(Continued)

Tests	Observations
4 Dilute nitric acid was added to the fourth portion of the solution followed by aqueous silver nitrate.	
5 Dilute nitric acid was added to the fifth portion of the solution and then aqueous barium nitrate.	
Tests on the residue	
Dilute hydrochloric acid was added to the residue.	rapid effervescence observed
The gas given off was tested.	limewater turned milky
Excess aqueous sodium hydroxide was added to the mixture in the test tube.	white precipitate, insoluble in excess

Table 12.03

ii   Name the gas given off in the tests on the residue.

    ....

iii What conclusions can you draw about solid **Q** from the observations made? Explain your reasoning.

    ....

    ....

Exercise C12.02 Chemical testing and evaluation

This exercise links various chemical tests with the skills of designing experiments so that they give clear answers to the questions raised about a particular sample. The exercise will familiarise you with some of the analytical tests and experimental methods. At the end of the exercise, there is a checklist on which you can assess how well you have understood the key features of this type of practical planning.

a Limestone and chalk are impure forms of calcium carbonate. Calcium carbonate reacts with hydrochloric acid to form calcium chloride, carbon dioxide and water.

You are provided with lumps of limestone and chalk and hydrochloric acid together with a full range of lab apparatus. Devise an experiment to discover which of these two types of rock contains the higher percentage of calcium carbonate.

....

....

....

....

....

....

....

....

b The label on a 500 ml bottle of **Harcourt Spring Water** states the following:

Harcourt Spring
Water

Composition mg/litre
calcium 55 mg
magnesium 16 mg
potassium 2 mg
sodium 15 mg
hydrogencarbonate 240 mg
sulfate 28 mg
nitrate 6 mg
chloride 11 mg

Dry residue after evaporation
255 mg
pH 4.6

i What are the formulae of the following ions?

Potassium ion: ....

Magnesium ion: ....

Nitrate ion: ....

Hydrogencarbonate ion: ....

ii Describe a test to confirm the presence of sodium ions in the water.

....

iii How could you confirm that the pH of the water was 4.6?

....

iv Describe how you could confirm the amount of dry residue given on the label.

....

....

....

....

....

c The metals magnesium, iron and zinc all react exothermically with hydrochloric acid to form chloride salts. For example:

$$\textbf{Zn} + 2HCl \longrightarrow \textbf{ZnCl}_2 + H_2$$

i How could you test a salt solution to show that it contained magnesium ions?

....

....

....

ii Describe an experiment, using the reaction of the metals with acid, which would place the three metals (magnesium, iron and zinc) in order of reactivity.

....

....

....

....

d You are provided with magnesium ribbon and sulfuric acid together with normal laboratory apparatus. Describe an experiment to show the effect of concentration on the rate of a chemical reaction.

....

....

....

....

....

....

....

Use the checklist below to give yourself a mark for your experiment planning. For each point, award yourself:

- **2 marks if you did it really well**
- **1 mark if you made a good attempt at it, and partly succeeded**
- **0 mark if you did not try to do it, or did not succeed.**

Self-assessment checklist for planning experiments:

Check point	Marks awarded	
	You	Your teacher
You have stated the variable to be changed (independent variable).		
You have stated the range of this variable you will use, and how you will vary it.		
You have stated at least three important variables to be kept constant (and not included ones that are not important).		
You have stated the variable to be measured (dependent variable), how you will measure it and when you will measure it.		
You have drawn up an outline results chart where appropriate.		
If a hypothesis is being tested, you have predicted what the results will be if the hypothesis is correct.		
Total (out of 12)		

10–12 Excellent.

8–9 Good.

5–7 A good start, but you need to improve quite a bit.

3–4 Poor. Try this same plan again.

1–2 Very poor. Read through all the criteria again, and then try the same plan again.

Exercise C12.03 Experimental design

> This exercise emphasises the considerations that are important when planning and evaluating an experimental method.

How is the rate of a reaction affected by temperature?

The reaction between dilute hydrochloric acid and sodium thiosulfate solution produces a fine yellow precipitate that clouds the solution (apparatus used shown in the diagram below). This means that the rate of this reaction can be found by measuring the time taken for a cross (×) under the reaction to become hidden.

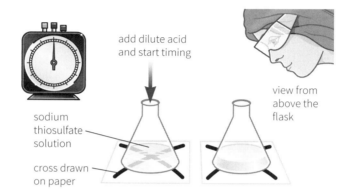

add dilute acid and start timing

view from above the flask

sodium thiosulfate solution

cross drawn on paper

121

a You are asked to design an experiment to see how changing the temperature of the solutions mixed affects the rate of the reaction.

You are provided with the following apparatus and solutions:

- several 100 cm³ conical flasks of the same size and shape

- dilute hydrochloric acid solution (0.5 mol/dm³)

- sodium thiosulfate solution – a colourless solution (0.5 mol/dm³)

- several 50 cm³ measuring cylinders

- a piece of white card and a felt-tip marker pen

- a stopclock

- a water bath that is thermostatically controlled so that the temperature can be adjusted – flasks of solution can be placed in this to adjust to the required temperature

- two thermometers

- and any other normal lab apparatus.

Your description should include:

- a statement of the **aim** of the experiment – comment on which factors in the experiment need to be kept constant and why

- a description of the **method** for carrying out the experiment – this should be a **list of instructions** to another student

- safety – put in a comment on what **safety precautions** you need to take and why.

....

....

....

....

....

....

b Below are the results of tests carried out at five different temperatures. In each case, 50 cm³ of aqueous sodium thiosulfate was poured into a flask. 10 cm³ of hydrochloric acid was added to the flask. The initial and final temperatures were measured.

Use the thermometer diagrams to record all of the initial and final temperatures in the table.

i Complete Table 12.04 to show the average temperatures.

Experiment	Thermometer diagram at start	Initial temperature / °C	Thermometer diagram at end	Final temperature / °C	Average temperature / °C	Time for cross to disappear / s
1		....		....	....	130
2		....		....	....	79
3		....		....	....	55
4		....		....	....	33
5		....		....	....	26

Table 12.04

ii Plot a graph of the time taken for the cross to disappear versus the average temperature on the grid provided, and draw a smooth line graph.

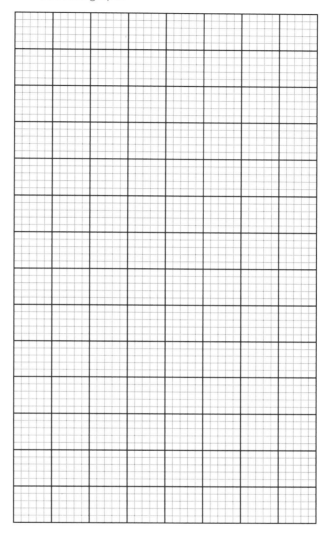

c In which experiment was the speed of reaction greatest? ....

d Explain why the speed was greatest in this experiment.

....

....

e Why were the same volume of sodium thiosulfate solution and the same volume of hydrochloric acid used in each experiment? Why do the conical flasks used in each test run need to be of the same dimensions?

....

....

f From the graph, deduce the time for the cross to disappear if the experiment was to be repeated at 70 °C. Show clearly on the grid how you worked out your answer.

....

g Sketch on the grid the curve you would expect if all the experiments were repeated using 50 cm³ of more concentrated sodium thiosulfate solution.

h How would it be possible to achieve a temperature of around 0 to 5 °C?

....

i Explain one change that could be made to the experimental method to obtain more accurate results.

....

Use the checklist below to give yourself a mark for your graph. For each point, award yourself:
- **2 marks if you did it really well**
- **1 mark if you made a good attempt at it, and partly succeeded**
- **0 marks if you did not try to do it, or did not succeed.**

Self-assessment checklist for graphs:

Check point	Marks awarded	
	You	Your teacher
You have drawn the axes with a ruler, using most of the width and height of the grid.		
You have used a good scale for the x-axis and the y-axis, going up in useful proportions.		
You have labelled the axes correctly, giving the correct units for the scales on both axes.		
You have plotted each point precisely and correctly.		
You have used a small, neat dot or cross for each point.		
You have drawn a single, clear best-fit line through the points – using a ruler for a straight line.		
You have ignored any anomalous results when drawing the line.		
Total (out of 14)		

12–14 Excellent.

10–11 Good.

7–9 A good start, but you need to improve quite a bit.

5–6 Poor. Try this same graph again, using a new sheet of graph paper.

1–4 Very poor. Read through all the criteria again, and then try the same graph again.

Example answers and all questions were written by the authors.

Chapter C1 Planet Earth

Exercise C1.01 Global warming and the 'greenhouse effect'

a Photosynthesis involves the 'capture' of energy from the Sun by the green leaves of plants and the synthesis of glucose. The green pigment, chlorophyll, is essential for this process. The conversion of carbon dioxide and water into glucose is represented by the following equation:

$$6CO_2 + 6H_2O \longrightarrow C_6H_{12}O_6 + 6O_2$$

b see diagram below

The Workbook suggests that this graph can be drawn more clearly on a larger sheet of graph paper. The data can also be usefully analysed using a computer graphing program such as Excel or Graphical Analysis – such programs allow curve fitting and extrapolation.

c There has been a steady increase in the level of carbon dioxide in the atmosphere since 1880. However, the curve has increased more sharply since the 1960s. This rate of increase has remained steady over recent decades.

d The trend in mean temperature is more variable – showing more peaks and troughs. However, since the 1940s the broad trend is for the mean temperature to increase (this broad trend is shown by the shaded area of extrapolation on the graph below; so your extrapolation should fit anywhere within this area).

e The graphs suggest that there might be a link (correlation) between the levels of CO_2 in the atmosphere and the Earth's mean temperature as the temperature graph shows similar changes to that of the carbon dioxide levels. However, this does not prove that an increase in carbon dioxide levels causes the temperature rise.

f If the current trends were to continue then they would suggest that CO_2 levels could reach 405–410 ppm in 2020, and around 450 ppm in 2040. The mean temperature could reach around 14.9 °C in 2020 and 15.4 °C in 2040.

g The rise seems to follow the Industrial Revolution and then the increase in energy generation and transport fuelled by fossil fuels.

h methane: cattle, cultivation of rice in paddy fields
nitrogen oxides: vehicle exhaust fumes from hot engines

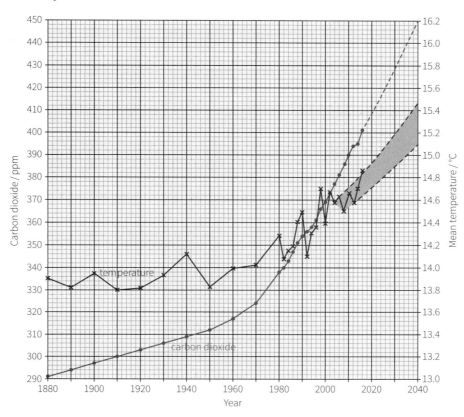

Exercise C1.02 Atmospheric pollution, industry and transport

a power stations

b coal, natural gas, petroleum (crude oil)

c flue gas desulfurisers (scrubbers)

d **i** $N_2 + O_2 \longrightarrow 2NO$

ii $2NO + O_2 \longrightarrow 2NO_2$

iii The level of NO_x in the emissions from a diesel-engined car would be higher because the increased operating temperature would result in more reaction between nitrogen and oxygen from the air.

iv a catalytic converter (catalyser)

e **i** The levels of these polluting gases would be higher in large cities because they are mainly produced by cars and other motor vehicles, and motor traffic is highest in large cities.

ii lead – because modern cars now use lead-free petrol (gasoline)

f **i** drop for 2002 = 13.4%
level at start of 2003 = 86.6% of original value
drop for 2003 = 5.2% of 86.6 = 4.5% of original
Total drop over two years = (13.4 + 4.5)% = 17.9%

ii No, the benefits take place in the initial years following the introduction of the charge but then the reduction will level out.

iii Changes in vehicle and engine technology, including the type of fuel used, e.g. the introduction of hybrid and electric-powered cars.

The Congestion Charge Zone is not an isolated area / pollution can enter the area by being blown in by the wind / changes in human activity within the Congestion Charge Zone will affect the levels of vehicle usage in the area.

g The transport of containers by road requires a large number of vehicles – this means that they can be delivered to a large number of different destinations but with a resultant high level of emissions, including carbon dioxide.

Transport by rail means that one locomotive can move a large number of containers – the level of emissions per container is less. There may need to be some road transport at the final destination but the distances involved, and therefore the level of emissions, would be less.

Exercise C1.03 Clean water is crucial

a Screens are used to filter away floating large items of rubbish (e.g. pieces of wood, logs, debris).

b Chlorine and/or ozone disinfect the water / they kill bacteria and microorganisms.

c Ozone breaks down/oxidises pesticides and other harmful chemicals.

d It is an oxidising agent.

e **i** the removal of salt(s) from solution

ii distillation, reverse osmosis

iii They are expensive, requiring large amounts of energy and sophisticated equipment.

f **i** test: acidify the tap water with a few drops of nitric acid and then add silver nitrate solution (or lead nitrate solution)

positive result: a white precipitate (of silver chloride) is seen

ii sodium chloride + silver nitrate
$\longrightarrow$ silver chloride + sodium nitrate
$NaCl + AgNO_3 \longrightarrow AgCl + NaNO_3$

iii $Ag^+(aq) + Cl^-(aq) \longrightarrow AgCl(s)$

Chapter C2 The nature of matter

Exercise C2.01 Changing physical state

a **A** solid   **B** solid and liquid (melting is in process)
C liquid   **D** liquid and gas (boiling is taking place)

b 17 °C

c 115 °C

d The temperature remains constant until the change of state is complete.

e The melting point and boiling point are not those of water.

f The kinetic model states that the ***particles*** in a liquid and a ***gas*** *are* in constant motion. In a gas, the particles are far apart from each other and their motion is said to be ***random***. The particles in a solid are held in fixed positions in a regular ***lattice***. In a solid, the particles can only ***vibrate*** about their fixed positions.

Liquids and gases are fluid states. When particles move in a fluid they can collide with each other. When they collide, they bounce off each other in ***different*** directions. If two gases or liquids are mixed the different types of particle ***spread*** out and get mixed up. This process is called ***diffusion***.

At the same ***temperature*** particles that have a lower mass move faster than those with higher mass. This means that the lighter particles will spread and mix more quickly; the lighter particles are said to ***diffuse*** faster than the heavier particles.

g i radon

ii radon and nitrogen

iii nitrogen

iv cobalt

v The sample of ethanoic acid is impure – the presence of impurities raises the boiling point of a substance.

Exercise C2.02 Plotting a cooling curve

a

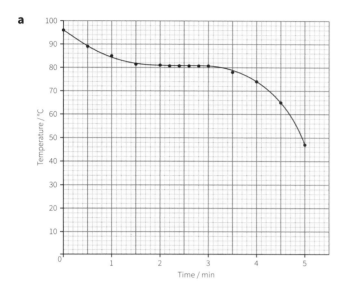

b The substance is freezing (solidifying) / turning from liquid to solid.

c The temperature stays constant because energy is being released as the substance solidifies / the molecules are giving out heat as they stop moving from place to place and become organised in a structured lattice arrangement / in the solid the molecules can only vibrate about fixed points / the heat released keeps the temperature constant until all the substance is solid.

d You would need to use an oil bath (in place of the water bath) so that the higher temperature could be reached.

e i

Temperature / °C

Time / min

ii The curve flattens but the temperature does not stay constant while the wax solidifies. This is because wax is a mixture of substances, not a pure compound.

f i Water ice has a film of liquid water on its surface; solid carbon dioxide is dry (no liquid film).

ii The carbon dioxide is under pressure in the fire extinguisher.

iii Hoar frost is a powdery **white** frost caused when solid **ice** forms from **humid** air. The solid surface on which it is formed must be **colder** than the **surrounding** air. Water vapour is deposited on a surface as fine ice **crystals** without going through the **liquid** phase.

Exercise C2.03 Diffusion, solubility and separation

a i The purple crystals are soluble in water so the water begins to break up the crystals, and particles (ions) from the solid move into the water. This continues until all the solid dissolves. The particles then move through the liquid and spread out through the liquid until the solution is evenly coloured throughout.

ii A shorter time – if the temperature was higher, the particles would be moving faster as they would have more energy / the process of diffusion would take place more quickly.

b i The analysis would be done by chromatography. A piece of filter paper (chromatography paper) would be set up with a pencil line drawn across the bottom, samples of the green solution would be spotted on the line and the bottom edge of the paper then dipped carefully in a solvent (e.g. ethanol). The solvent would rise up the paper and different substances would move at different rates up the paper. One spot would be chlorophyll (green), but other (yellow) spots would be seen.

ii

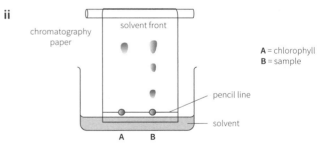

iii Photosynthesis is an endothermic process. Chlorophyll captures energy from the Sun which is then used to bring about the reaction between carbon dioxide and water to make glucose. Oxygen is a by-product of the reaction.

carbon dioxide + water $\rightarrow$ glucose + oxygen

$$6CO_2 + 6H_2O \rightarrow C_6H_{12}O_6 + 6O_2$$

c

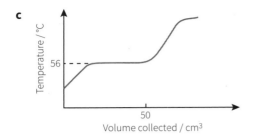

Exercise C2.04 Chromatography at the races

a Two factors:
  - the length of time the chromatogram is run (developed) for
  - the solubility of the substance in the solvent – the more soluble the substance, the further it runs

b Horse **C**; paracetamol

c It is used as a painkiller.

d $R_f = \dfrac{\text{distance travelled by the substance}}{\text{distance travelled by the solvent}} = \dfrac{7.5}{10.0} = 0.75$

Note that you have a partial check on your answer here as the R_f value must be less than 1.

Exercise C2.05 Atomic structure

a Atoms are made up of three different particles: **protons** which are positively charged; **neutrons** which have no charge; and **electrons** which are negatively charged. The negatively charged particles are arranged in different **energy levels** (shells) around the **nucleus** of the atom. The particles with a negligible mass are the **electrons**.

All atoms of the same element contain the same number of **protons** and **electrons**. Atoms of the same element with different numbers of **neutrons** *are* known as **isotopes**.

b The electrons in an atom are arranged in a series of **shells** around the nucleus. These shells are also called **energy** levels. In an atom, the shell **nearest** to the nucleus fills first, then the next shell, and so on. There is room for
  - up to **two** electrons in the first shell
  - up to **eight** electrons in the second shell
  - up to **eight** electrons in the third shell.

(There are 18 electrons in total when the three shells are completely full.)

The elements in the Periodic Table are organised in the same way as the electrons fill the shells. Shells fill from **left** to **right** across the **rows** of the Periodic Table.
  - The first shell fills up first from **hydrogen** to helium.
  - The second shell fills next from lithium to **neon**.
  - Eight **electrons** go into the third shell from sodium to argon.
  - Then the fourth shell starts to fill from potassium.

c **i** 38

  ii 53

  iii 137 − 55 = 82

Exercise C2.06 Influential organisation

a **i** see Table A2.01

  ii The chemical properties of isotopes of the same element are the same because the number and arrangement of electrons in the isotopes are the same / the atoms of the isotopes all have the same number of outer electrons.

Isotope	Name of element	Proton number	Nucleon number	Number of		
				p	n	e
$^{12}_{6}C$	carbon	6	12	6	6	6
$^{14}_{6}C$	*carbon*	6	*14*	6	8	6
$^{1}_{1}H$	*hydrogen*	*1*	1	*1*	0	*1*
$^{3}_{1}H$	hydrogen (tritium)	*1*	*3*	*1*	*2*	*1*
$^{31}_{15}P$	*phosphorus*	15	31	*15*	*16*	*15*
$^{32}_{15}P$	*phosphorus*	*15*	*32*	*15*	*17*	*15*
$^{127}_{53}I$	iodine	*53*	*127*	53	*74*	*53*
$^{131}_{53}I$	*iodine*	*53*	*131*	53	*78*	*53*

Table A2.01

128

b see Table A2.02

Atom	Proton number	Electron arrangement			
		1st shell	2nd shell	3rd shell	4th shell
A	2	2			
B	5	2	3		
C	13	2	8	3	
D	15	2	8	5	
E	19	2	8	8	1

Table A2.02

i one (**B**)

ii **B** and **C**

iii three

iv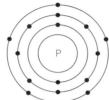

b carbon and silicon

c Group IV

d • The halogens are ~~metals~~ / **non-metals** and their vapours are **coloured** / ~~colourless~~.
• The halogens are **toxic** / ~~non-toxic~~ to humans.
• Halogen molecules are each made of ~~one~~ / **two** atoms; they are ~~monatomic~~ / **diatomic**.
• Halogens react with **metal** / ~~non-metal~~ elements to form crystalline compounds that are salts.
• The halogens get ~~more~~ / **less** reactive going down the group in the Periodic Table.
• Halogens can ~~colour~~ / **bleach** vegetable dyes and kill bacteria.

e

Name of element	sulfur	selenium	tellurium
density / g/cm³	2.07	*4.79*	6.24
melting point / °C	115	221	*450*
boiling point / °C	445	*685*	988
ionic radius / nm	0.184	*0.198*	*0.221*

Table A3.01

Chapter C3 Elements and compounds

Exercise C3.01 Periodic patterns in the properties of the elements

a

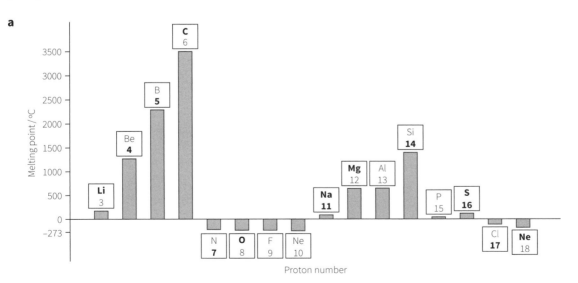

Exercise C3.02 The first four periods

a lithium and sodium (Li, Na)

b chromium and copper (Cr, Cu)

c helium (He)

d bromine (Br)

e carbon (C)

f sulfur (S)

g helium, neon and krypton (He, Ne, Kr)

h copper (Cu)

i calcium (Ca)

j magnesium (Mg)

Exercise C3.03 Trends in the halogens

a

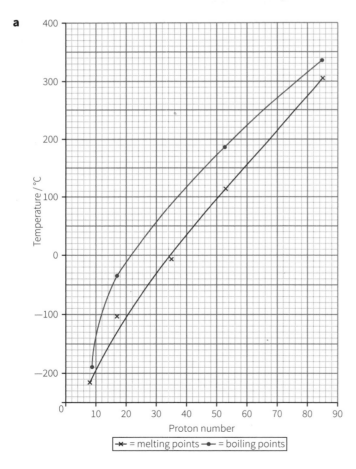

Proton number

─✳─ = melting points ─•─ = boiling points

b estimated boiling point = 95–115 °C (actual value 114 °C)

colour: red-brown

physical state: liquid

c fluorine and chlorine

d solid, black

e The melting points increase as you go down the group.

Exercise C3.04 The chemical bonding in simple molecules

a see diagrams below

Name of compound	Formula	Drawing of structure	Molecular model
hydrogen chloride	**HCl**	H─Cl	
water	H_2O	H─O─H	
ammonia	**NH₃**	H─N─H with H below	
methane	CH_4	H─C─H with H above and below	
ethene	C_2H_4	H₂C=CH₂	
carbon dioxide	CO_2	O=C=O	

b • The strong bonds between the atoms are **covalent** bonds.

• In the crystal, there are two oxygen atoms for every silicon atom, so the formula is **SiO_2**.

• The atoms of the lattice are organised in a **tetrahedral** arrangement like diamond, with a silicon atom at the centre of each **tetrahedron (pyramid)**.

• This is an example of a **giant molecular (covalent)** structure.

- Each oxygen atom forms **two** covalent bonds.
- Each silicon atom forms **four** covalent bonds.

c i Graphite conducts electricity because not all of the outer electrons of the carbon atoms are used in the covalent bonding that holds the atoms together in the layers. These 'free' electrons are able to move in between the layers. They can be made to move in one direction when a voltage is applied.

ii Graphite acts as a lubricant because there are only weak forces between the layers of carbon atoms in the structure. The layers can be made to move over each other if a force is applied.

Exercise C3.05 Formulae of ionic compounds

a i CuO

ii Na_2CO_3

iii $ZnSO_4$

iv $AgNO_3$

v $MgBr_2$

vi $(NH_4)_2SO_4$

vii Mg_3N_2

viii K_3PO_4

ix $Fe(OH)_3$

x $CrCl_3$

b i 1 : 1

ii 1 : 2

iii 3 : 2

iv 1 : 3 : 3

v 2 : 8 : 1 : 4

c i 2 : 1

ii K_2O

d i

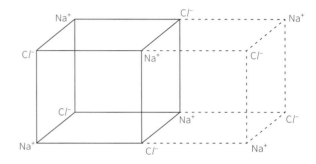

ii

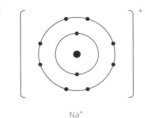 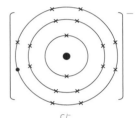

iii see diagram below

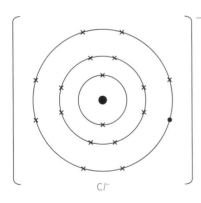 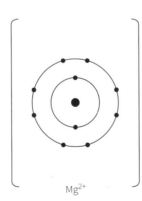 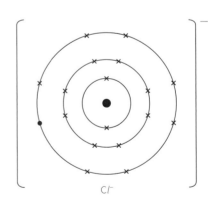

Exercise C3.06 The bonding in covalent molecules

See Table A3.02

Molecule	Dot-and-cross diagram	Structure
Ammonia (NH$_3$)	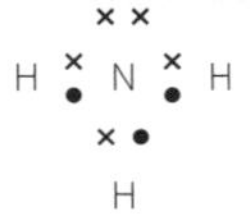	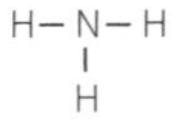 H−N−H with H below N
Water (H$_2$O)	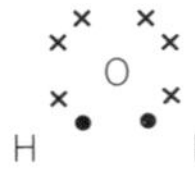	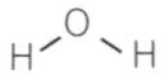 H−O−H (bent)
Hydrogen chloride (HCl)	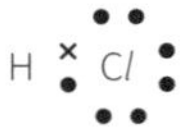	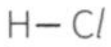 H−Cl
Ethane (C$_2$H$_6$)	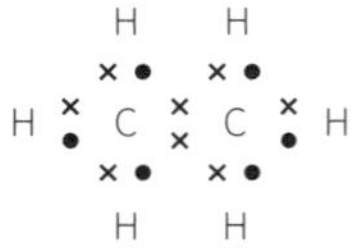	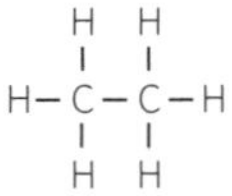 H−C−C−H with H above and below each C
Ethene (C$_2$H$_4$)	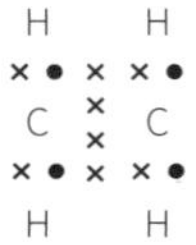	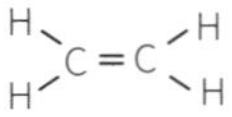 C=C with H atoms
Ethanol (C$_2$H$_5$OH)	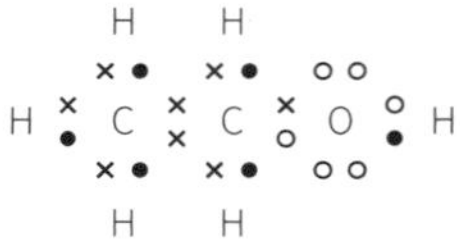	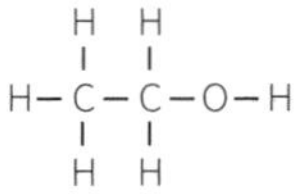 H−C−C−O−H with H above and below each C

Table A3.02

Exercise C3.07 The nature of ionic lattices

Property	Explanation
The solution of an ionic compound in water is a good conductor of electricity – such ionic substances are electrolytes.	The ions in the giant ionic structure are always arranged in the same regular way – see the diagram.
Ionic crystals have a regular shape. All the crystals of each solid ionic compound are the same shape. Whatever the size of the crystal, the angles between the faces of the crystal are always the same.	The giant ionic structure is held together by the strong attraction between the positive and negative ions. It takes a lot of energy to break down the regular arrangement of ions.
Ionic compounds have relatively high melting points.	In a molten ionic compound, the positive and negative ions can move around – they can move to the electrodes when a voltage is applied.
When an ionic compound is heated above its melting point, the molten compound is a good conductor of electricity.	In a solution of an ionic compound, the positive metal ions and the negative non-metal ions can move around – they can move to the electrodes when a voltage is applied.

Exercise C3.08 Giant molecular lattices

a Silicon(IV) oxide occurs naturally as ~~mud~~ /**sand**. It has a giant **covalent** / ~~electrostatic~~ structure very similar to ~~graphite~~ /**diamond**. Such a structure can also be described as a ~~micromolecule~~ / **macromolecule** as all the atoms in the crystal are joined together by covalent bonds.

Each silicon atom is bonded to **four** / ~~two~~ oxygen atoms, while each oxygen atom is linked covalently to ~~four~~ / **two** silicon atoms. The oxygen atoms are arranged ~~hexagonally~~ /**tetrahedrally** around the silicon atoms.

The fact that all the atoms are bonded together in a ~~two-dimensional~~ /**three-dimensional** structure like ~~graphite~~ / **diamond** means that silicon(IV) oxide has similar physical properties to ~~graphite~~ / **diamond**. Silica is **very hard** / ~~slippery~~ and has a a ~~low~~ / **high** melting point. All the outer electrons of the atoms are used in making the covalent bonds between the atoms. This means that silicon(IV) oxide ~~does~~ /**does not** conduct electricity. There are no electrons free to carry the current through the crystal.

b see Table A3.03

Observation	Explanation
Diamond and silica are both very hard substances...	... because all the atoms in the structure are joined by strong covalent bonds
Diamond does not conduct electricity...	... because **all the outer electrons of the atoms are involved in making bonds**
Graphite is **slippery**...	... because the layers in the structure are only held together by weak forces
Graphite conducts electricity...	... because there are some free electrons that are able to move between the layers to carry the current

Table A3.03

Exercise C3.09 Making magnesium oxide – a quantitative investigation

a The mass of magnesium oxide produced increases if more magnesium is used. The increase is linear (directly proportional).

b

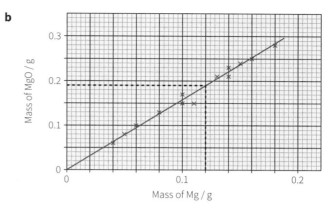

mass of MgO produced = 0.19 g

Note that your answer may differ slightly because your line of best fit may be slightly different. A sensible range of answers would be allowed in the exam.

c 0.19 − 0.12 = 0.07 g

d $\dfrac{0.07}{0.12} \times 24 = 14$ g

e from the experiment: see Table A3.04

	Mg	O
mass	24	14
number of moles	$\dfrac{24}{24} = 1.0$	$\dfrac{14}{16} = 0.88$
whole number ratio	1	1

Table A3.04

The ratio of moles of Mg to moles of O is 1 : 1

so the formula is MgO.

133

Chapter C4 Chemical reactions

Exercise C4.01 Key chemical reactions

a

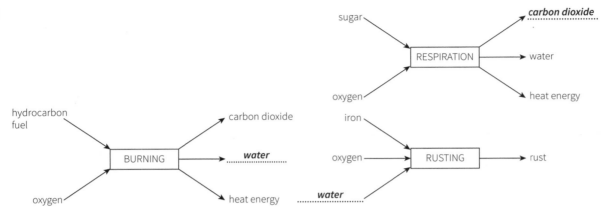

b oxidation

c • If a substance **gains** oxygen during a reaction, it is **oxidised**.

  • If a substance **loses** oxygen during a reaction, it is **reduced**.

d i copper(II) oxide + hydrogen $\xrightarrow{\text{heat}}$ copper + water

$$CuO + H_2 \xrightarrow{\text{heat}} Cu + H_2O$$

with *oxidation* bracket above CuO → Cu and *reduction* bracket below H₂ → H₂O

ii Hydrogen is acting as a reducing agent (reductant).

e i • Oxidation is the **loss** of electrons.
  • Reduction is the **gain** of electrons.

ii

$$Zn(s) + Cu^{2+}(aq) \rightarrow Zn^{2+}(aq) + Cu(s)$$

with *reduction* bracket above and *oxidation* bracket below

iii Copper(II) ions are acting as an oxidising agent.

Exercise C4.02 The action of heat on metal carbonates

a thermal decomposition

b carbon dioxide; the test is to bubble the gas into limewater, and the limewater will turn milky if the gas is carbon dioxide (a white precipitate is produced)

c see Table A4.01

Metal	Name of metal
A	copper
B	magnesium
C	calcium
D	sodium
E	zinc

Table A4.01

d $ZnCO_3 \rightarrow ZnO + CO_2$

Exercise C4.03 The nature of electrolysis

Changes taking place during electrolysis

During electrolysis ionic compounds are decomposed by the passage of an electric current. For this to happen, the compound must be either **molten** or in **solution**. Electrolysis can occur when an electric **current** passes through a molten **electrolyte**. The two rods dipping into the electrolyte are called the **electrodes**. In this situation, metals are deposited at the **cathode** and non-metals are formed at the **anode**.

134

When the ionic compound is dissolved in water, the electrolysis can be more complex. Generally, during electrolysis **positive** ions move towards the **cathode** and negative ions move towards the **anode**. At the negative electrode (cathode) the metal or **hydrogen** ions gain electrons and form metal atoms or hydrogen **molecules**. At the positive electrode (anode) certain non-metal ions **lose** electrons and **oxygen** or chlorine is produced.

Examples of electrolysis in industry

There are several important industrial applications of electrolysis; the most important economically being the electrolysis of **molten** aluminium oxide to produce aluminium. The aluminium oxide is mixed with molten **cryolite** to **lower** the melting point of the electrolyte.

A **concentrated** aqueous solution of sodium chloride contains **sodium**, chloride, hydrogen and **hydroxide** ions. When this solution is electrolysed, **hydrogen** rather than sodium is discharged at the negative electrode. The solution remaining is sodium hydroxide.

When a solution of copper(II) sulfate is electrolysed using **copper** electrodes, an unusual thing happens and the copper atoms of the **positive** electrode (anode) go into solution as copper ions. At the cathode the copper ions turn into copper atoms, and the metal is deposited on this electrode. This can be used as a method of refining or **purifying** impure copper.

Exercise C4.04 Displacement reactions of the halogens

a   see Table A4.02

b   iodine $\longrightarrow$ bromine $\longrightarrow$ chlorine
$\xrightarrow{}$
        increasing reactivity

Exercise C4.05 Self-heating cans, hand warmers and cool packs

Self-heating cans

a   an exothermic reaction

b   The chemicals might burst their container and mix with the food/drink.

c   by leaving an empty space above the chemicals

d   calcium oxide + water $\longrightarrow$ calcium hydroxide

   $CaO + H_2O \longrightarrow Ca(OH)_2$

e   Limestone (calcium carbonate) is heated strongly in a lime kiln.

   $CaCO_3 \longrightarrow CaO + CO_2$

f   Any **two** from the following:
   - copper sulfate, zinc and water
   - calcium chloride and water
   - magnesium, iron and water

Heat pads and hand warmers

a   oxygen from the air

b Fe_2O_3

c $4Fe + 3O_2 + 2xH_2O \longrightarrow 2Fe_2O_3 \cdot xH_2O$

d   The presence of salt speeds up the rusting reaction.

Test solution	Add chlorine water; followed by hexane	Add bromine water; followed by hexane	Add aqueous iodine; followed by hexane
KCl(aq)		no reaction	no reaction
KBr(aq)	solution changes from colourless to brown; brown colour moves into hexane layer		no reaction
KI(aq)	solution changes from colourless to brown; purple colour moves into hexane layer	solution changes from colourless to brown; purple colour moves into hexane layer	

Table A4.02

e i a super-saturated solution

    ii The hand warmer is placed in hot water to heat it and re-dissolve the sodium thiosulfate.

    iii No, once the rusting reaction has taken place it is not easy to reverse the reaction so that type of hand warmer is not re-usable.

Cool packs

a as a fertiliser (is also used as an explosive)

b advantage: can be used anywhere instantly
disadvantage: cannot be re-used

c Take a measured amount of water, take the temperature and then add a series of known masses of ammonium nitrate. Take the temperature after each addition.

Plot a graph to show temperature change against mass of ammonium nitrate added – then read off from the graph the mass needed to reduce temperature to 5 °C.

Other methods are possible but they must work.

Exercise C4.06 The movement of ions

a Manganate(VI) ions are purple.

b The manganate ions are negatively charged (MnO_4^-) and so they move towards the positive terminal.

c anions (negative ions): manganate (MnO_4^-), sulfate (SO_4^{2-})
cations (positive ions): potassium (K^+), copper (Cu^{2+})

d Copper manganate contains blue copper ions and purple manganate ions. The positively charged copper ions would move towards the negative terminal and the purple manganate ions would move towards the positive terminal. We would see blue and purple spots moving in opposite directions.

Exercise C4.07 Making and 'breaking' copper chloride

Synthesising copper(II) chloride

a malleable and ductile

b green

c Chlorine gas is toxic (poisonous).

d exothermic – there is a flame produced / the metal film flares as it reacts

The fact that the metal is a thin sheet means that it has a large surface area to react with the chlorine gas.

e The pale blue-green colour of the solution suggests that a copper(II) salt has been produced.

f $Cu + Cl_2 \longrightarrow CuCl_2$

g zinc chloride

Decomposing copper(II) chloride

a copper(II) chloride $\longrightarrow$ copper + chlorine
$CuCl_2 \longrightarrow Cu + Cl_2$

b Electrolysis is the breakdown of an ionic compound, molten or in aqueous solution, by the passage of electricity.

c A piece of damp (moist) litmus paper is held in the gas: it is bleached white.

d i It must be carried out in a fume cupboard.

    ii Dip a piece of litmus paper in the solution around the positive electrode: it will be bleached because chlorine is soluble in water.

e endothermic – electrical energy is used to split the compound into its elements

f at the anode: $2Cl^- (aq) \longrightarrow Cl_2(g) + 2e^-$
at the cathode: $Cu^{2+}(aq) + 2e^- \longrightarrow Cu(s)$

Chapter C5 Acids, bases and salts

Exercise C5.01 Acid and base reactions – neutralisation

All salts are ionic compounds. Salts are produced when an alkali neutralises an *acid*. In this reaction, the salt is formed when a *metallic* ion or an ammonium ion from the alkali replaces one or more *hydrogen* ions of the acid.

Salts can be crystallised from the solution produced by the neutralisation reaction. The salt crystals formed often contain *water* of crystallisation. These salts are called *hydrated* salts. The salt crystals can be heated to drive off the *water* of crystallisation. The salt remaining is said to be *anhydrous*.

Salts can be made by other reactions of acids. Magnesium sulfate can be made by reacting magnesium carbonate with *sulfuric* acid. The gas given off is *carbon dioxide*. Water is also formed in this reaction.

All *sodium* salts are soluble in water.

Exercise C5.02 Types of salt

a i Hydrochloric acid always produces **chlorides**.

ii Nitric acid always produces **nitrates**.

iii Ethanoic acid always produces **ethanoates**.

b see Table A5.01

Substances reacted together		Salt produced	Other products of the reaction
dilute hydrochloric acid	zinc oxide	*zinc chloride*	*water*
dilute sulfuric acid	*copper carbonate*	copper sulfate	water and carbon dioxide
dilute sulfuric acid	*magnesium carbonate*	magnesium sulfate	water and carbon dioxide
dilute hydrochloric acid	*magnesium*	magnesium chloride	hydrogen
dilute nitric acid	copper oxide	*copper nitrate*	*water*
dilute ethanoic acid	*sodium hydroxide*	sodium ethanoate	water

Table A5.01

Exercise C5.03 Antacids

a i $MgCO_3 + 2HCl \longrightarrow MgCl_2 + H_2O + CO_2$

ii $Mg(OH)_2 + 2HCl \longrightarrow MgCl_2 + H_2O$

b because the reaction produces a gas, carbon dioxide, which would need to escape from the stomach

c i sodium carbonate and sodium hydrogencarbonate

ii because they can dissolve in the fluid in the stomach and so react more quickly with the acid

d It forms a barrier layer stopping the acid from rising out of the stomach.

Exercise C5.04 Fire extinguishers

a i 3, because two moles / molecules of carbon dioxide are produced for each mole / molecule of acid

ii 2, because there is only sufficient acid present to produce half a mole / molecule of carbon dioxide

b any two from water, foam, dry powder

Note how the extinguishers chosen work and the type of fire they are useful for:

- water works by cooling – for small-scale wood and paper fires (not suitable for flammable liquid or electrical fires)

- foam works by cutting off oxygen supply – for paper / wood / petrol / oil fires

- dry powder works by cutting off oxygen supply – for all types of fire.

c dry powder because it can be used safely on all types of fire

Exercise C5.05 Descaling a coffee machine

a calcium carbonate + hydrochloric acid
$\longrightarrow$ calcium chloride + water + carbon dioxide

$CaCO_3 + 2HCl \longrightarrow CaCl_2 + H_2O + CO_2$

b calcium citrate

c i Hydrochloric acid is too strong and may attack the metal of the machine.

ii Ethanoic acid may leave a taste of vinegar in the coffee.

d i H_3NSO_3. It is used as a descaler and rust remover.

ii 'Hard water' occurs in some areas, depending on the minerals present in the rocks in the area. It contains high levels of calcium or magnesium hydrogencarbonates. Mention of limestone areas. On heating, the calcium hydrogencarbonate decomposes to give insoluble calcium carbonate (limescale).

Exercise C5.06 The analysis of titration results

See Table A5.02

Burette readings / cm³	Experiment 1	Experiment 2
final reading	*10.6*	*36.1*
initial reading	0.0	*14.9*
difference	*10.6*	*21.2*

Table A5.02

a neutralisation

b hydrochloric acid + sodium hydroxide
$\longrightarrow$ sodium chloride + water

c yellow $\longrightarrow$ red

d Experiment **2**

e More acid used in Experiment **2** to neutralise the same volume of sodium hydroxide, so acid solution in this experiment must be a more dilute solution. Twice as much acid used, so this acid solution must be half the concentration of that used in Experiment **1** (solution **P**).

f volume of solution **P** needed = 2.5 × 10.6 = 26.5 cm³
explanation: using 25.0 cm³ of sodium hydroxide instead of 10 cm³ so will need $\dfrac{25}{10}$ = 2.5 times the volume of acid to neutralise

g Use a pipette rather than a measuring cylinder.

Exercise C5.07 Thermochemistry – investigating the neutralisation of an acid by an alkali

A see Table A5.03

Volume of added NaOH(aq) / cm³	Temperature recorded / °C
0	21.0
10	28.0
20	35.0
30	35.0
40	31.0
50	30.0
60	27.5

Table A5.03

b and **c**

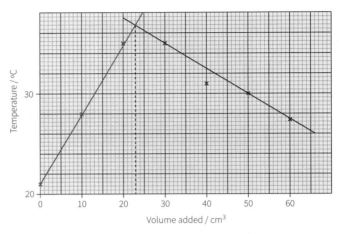

d the temperature after adding 40 cm³ of acid

e 23 cm³ (22.0–24.0 cm³ depending on lines drawn); it is the point where the two extrapolated lines meet

f The solutions are left to stand so that they are both at the same starting temperature (room temperature).

g Polystyrene is a good insulator and does not let heat from the reaction escape to the surroundings. It is a better insulator than glass.

h Improvements:
- the solutions could be more accurately measured out using a pipette or burette
- a more accurate thermometer could be used (one that reads to 0.1 °C)
- more values could be taken so that the graph could be more accurately drawn
- could use a lid on the polystyrene beaker to help retain heat (any three of these, and other sensible suggestions)

i sodium hydroxide + nitric acid $\longrightarrow$ sodium nitrate + water

$NaOH + HNO_3 \longrightarrow NaNO_3 + H_2O$

j exothermic

k $1.0 \times \dfrac{25.0}{1000} = 0.025$

l from equation: 1 mole of sodium hydroxide reacts with 1 mole of nitric acid, therefore 0.025 moles NaOH will react with **0.025 moles of nitric acid**

m from experiment: there are 0.025 moles of acid in 23.0 cm³ of solution concentration of acid solution = $0.025 \times \dfrac{1000}{23.0} = 1.09$

mol/dm³ = **1.1 mol/dm³** (to two significant figures)

138

Chapter C6 Quantitative chemistry

Exercise C6.01 Calculating formula masses

a

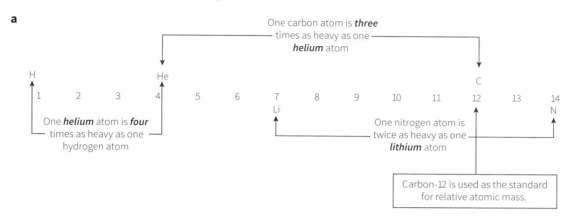

b see Table A6.01

Molecule	Chemical formula	Number of atoms or ions involved	Relative formula mass
oxygen	O_2	2 O	$2 \times 16 = 32$
carbon dioxide	CO_2	1 C and 2 O	$1 \times 12 + 2 \times 16 = 44$
water	H_2O	2 H and 1 *O*	$2 \times 1 + 16 = 18$
ammonia	NH_3	1 N and 3 H	$14 + 3 \times 1 = 17$
calcium carbonate	$CaCO_3$	$1 Ca^{2+}$ and $1 CO_3^{2-}$	$40 + 12 + 3 \times 16 = 100$
magnesium oxide	MgO	$1 Mg^{2+}$ and $1 O^{2-}$	$1 \times 24 + 1 \times 16 = 40$
ammonium nitrate	NH_4NO_3	$1 NH_4^+$ and *$1 NO_3^-$*	$2 \times 14 + 4 \times 1 + 3 \times 16 = 80$
propanol	C_3H_7OH	3 C, *8 H* and *1 O*	$3 \times 12 + 8 \times 1 + 1 \times 16 = 60$

Table A6.01

Exercise C6.02 A sense of proportion in chemistry

a 5 tonnes zinc oxide $\rightarrow$ 4 tonnes zinc

so 20 tonnes zinc oxide $\rightarrow 4 \times \dfrac{20}{5} = $ **16 tonnes zinc**

or $\dfrac{4}{5} = \dfrac{x}{20}$ so $x = 4 \times \dfrac{20}{5} = 16$ tonnes of zinc

b 17 tonnes of ammonia are produced from 14 tonnes nitrogen so 34 tonnes of ammonia will be produced

from $14 \times \dfrac{34}{17} = $ **28 tonnes of nitrogen**

or $\dfrac{14}{17} = \dfrac{x}{34}$ so $x = 14 \times \dfrac{34}{17} = 28$ tonnes of nitrogen

c 12 C atoms + 22 H atoms + 11 O atoms = 45 atoms

d $C_2H_4O_2$

Exercise C6.03 Calculations involving solutions

a i

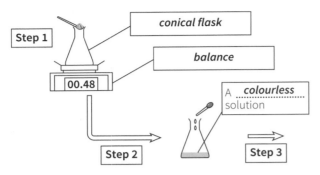

ii   see Table A6.02

Final burette reading / cm³	14.60
First burette reading / cm³	0.20
Volume of NaOH(aq) added / cm³	**14.40** (P)

Table A6.02

b *1st stage*:

- 14.40 cm³ of NaOH(aq) containing 0.50 moles in 1000 cm³ were used.

- Number of moles NaOH used = $\dfrac{0.5}{1000} \times$ **14.40** = **7.20 × 10⁻³** moles (or 0.0072 moles)

2nd stage:

- Note that 1 mole of citric acid reacts with 3 moles of sodium hydroxide.
- Number of moles citric acid in sample = $\dfrac{7.20 \times 10^{-3}}{3} \times$ **2.40 × 10⁻³** moles (or 0.0024 moles)

3rd stage:

- Relative formula mass of citric acid (M_r of $C_6H_8O_7$) = **192**

- Mass of citric acid in sample = **2.40 × 10⁻³ × 192 = 0.46** g

- Percentage purity of sample = $\dfrac{0.46}{0.48} \times 100$ = **95.8%**

  Note that you have a clue that you are on the right lines in your calculation because your value for the mass of citric acid must be less than 0.48 g.

c The citric acid can be further purified by re-crystallisation.

d • Number of moles of H_2SO_4 in 25.00 cm³ of 2.0 mol/dm⁻³ solution = **(2.0/1000) × 25 = 0.05 moles**

- Maximum number of moles of $CuSO_4 \cdot 5H_2O$ that could be formed = **0.05 moles**

- Maximum mass of crystals, $CuSO_4 \cdot 5H_2O$, that could be formed = **0.05 × 250 = 12.5 g**

  (The mass of 1 mole of $CuSO_4 \cdot 5H_2O$ is 250 g.)

- Percentage yield = (7.3/12.5) × 100 = **58.4%**

Exercise C6.04 Finding the mass of 5 cm of magnesium ribbon

a see Table A6.03

Experiment number	Volume of hydrogen collected / cm³
1	85
2	79
3	82
average	**82**

Table A6.03

The results are not equal because of the difficulty in cutting exactly equal lengths of magnesium ribbon. Also the pieces of ribbon may not be exactly the same thickness or width, or gas may be lost as the magnesium is allowed to fall into the flask, or there may have been air in the measuring cylinder before starting.

b from equation: 24 g of magnesium (1 mole) $\rightarrow$ 24 000 cm³ of hydrogen so 1 cm³ of hydrogen produced from 24/24 000 = 0.001 g of magnesium and 82 cm³ of hydrogen produced from 0.001 × 82 = **0.082 g**

c 24 g of magnesium $\rightarrow$ 120 g of magnesium sulfate so 0.082 g will give (120/24) × 0.082 **= 0.41 g**

The answers to **b** and **c** could be calculated by other proportionality methods.

d The key factor here is that 24 g of magnesium will produce 120 g of dried anhydrous magnesium sulfate ($MgSO_4$) (see the equation).

- Weigh out a known mass of magnesium ribbon.
- React it with excess dilute sulfuric acid until no more gas is given off and no magnesium remains.
- Transfer the solution to a beaker of known mass.

- Heat the solution to dryness, taking care to avoid spitting.
- Allow to cool and weigh the beaker and residue.
- Filter, dry and weigh the crystals carefully.
- From the data above, calculate the mass of crystals that 5 cm would have given.

Exercise C6.05 Reacting volumes of gases

a 75 cm³

b 25 cm³

c 50 cm³

d $2NO$ + O_2 → $2NO_2$
50 cm³   25 cm³   50 cm³

Exercise C6.06 Calculation triangles

a see Table A6.04 and diagram below.

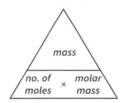

Substance	A_r or M_r	Number of moles	Mass / g
Cu	64	2	128
Mg	24	0.5	12
Cl_2	71	0.5	35.5
H_2	2	2	4
S_8	256	2	512
O_3	48	0.033	1.6
H_2SO_4	98	2.5	245
CO_2	44	0.4	17.6
NH_3	17	1.5	25.5
$CaCO_3$	100	1	100
$MgSO_4 \cdot 7H_2O$	246	0.33	82

Table A6.04

B see Table A6.05 and diagram below

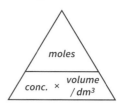

Solute	Volume of solution	Concentration of solution / mol/dm³	Moles of solute present
sodium chloride	1 dm³	0.5	0.5
hydrochloric acid	500 cm³	0.5	0.25
sodium hydroxide	2 dm³	0.5	1
sulfuric acid	250 cm³	2	0.5
sodium thiosulfate	200 cm³	2	0.4
copper(II) sulfate	7.5 dm³	0.1	0.75

Table A6.05

141

Exercise C6.07 Scaling up!

a i from equation: 1 mol Fe_2O_3 gives 2 mol Fe
100 g of Fe = 100/56 mol = 1.79 mol
mol of Fe_2O_3 needed = 1.79/2 = 0.895 mol
M_r of Fe_2O_3 = (56 × 2) + (16 × 3) = 160
mass of Fe_2O_3 needed = 0.895 × 160 = **143.2 g**
100 g of iron is **1.79** moles of Fe, so **0.895** moles of Fe_2O_3 are needed for the reaction, or **143.2 g** of iron(III) oxide

ii from above: 143.2 g Fe_2O_3 gives 100 g of Fe
so 143.2 tonnes Fe_2O_3 gives 100 tonnes of Fe
therefore **71.6 tonnes** of Fe_2O_3 are needed to produce 50 tonnes of Fe

b i $CaCO_3$ → $CaO + CO_2$

ii 1 mol $CaCO_3$ gives 1 mol CaO (quicklime)
100 g $CaCO_3$ gives 56 g CaO
or
100 tonnes $CaCO_3$ gives 56 tonnes CaO
1 tonne $CaCO_3$ gives 56/100 tonnes CaO
56/100 tonnes CaO = **0.56 tonnes**

Chapter C7   How far? How fast?

Exercise C7.01   Terms of reaction

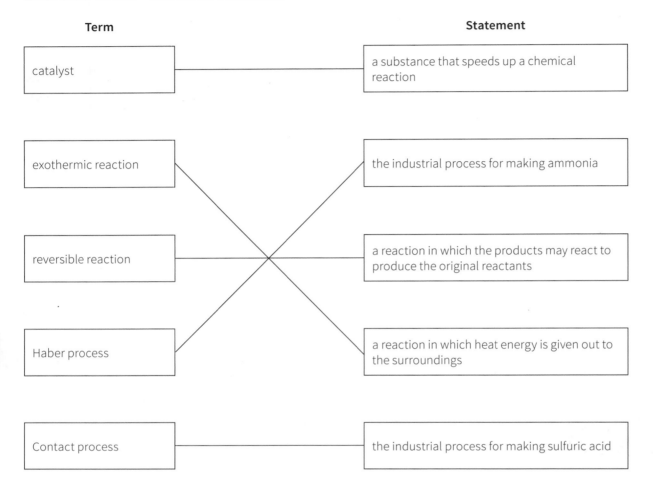

Term		Statement

catalyst — a substance that speeds up a chemical reaction

exothermic reaction

reversible reaction

Haber process

Contact process

the industrial process for making ammonia

a reaction in which the products may react to produce the original reactants

a reaction in which heat energy is given out to the surroundings

the industrial process for making sulfuric acid

Exercise C7.02   Energy diagrams

a   In an exothermic reaction, the **reactants** have more energy than the **products**. This means that ΔH is **negative**. The difference in energy is **given out** as heat.

The temperature of the surroundings **increases** / ~~decreases~~.

b   In an endothermic reaction, the **products** have more energy than the **reactants**. This means that ΔH is **positive**. The difference in energy is **taken in** from the surroundings.

The temperature of the surroundings ~~increases~~ / **decreases**.

Exercise C7.03 The collision theory of reaction rates

See Table A7.01

Factor affecting the reaction	Types of reaction affected	Change made in the condition	Effect on rate of reaction
concentration	all reactions involving solutions or reactions involving gases	an increase in the concentration of one, or both, of the **reactants (reacting substances)** means there are more particles in the same volume	increases the rate of reaction as the particles **collide** more frequently
pressure	reactions involving **gases** only	an increase in the pressure	greatly **increases** the rate of reaction – the effect is the same as that of an increase in **concentration**
temperature	all reactions	an increase in temperature – this means that molecules are moving **faster** and collide more **often (frequently)**; the particles also have more **energy** when they collide	**increases** the rate of reaction
particle size	reactions involving solids and liquids, solids and gases or mixtures of solids	use the same mass of a solid but make pieces of solid **more powdered (more broken up)**	greatly increases the rate of reaction
light	a number of photochemical reactions including photosynthesis, the reaction between methane and chlorine, and the reaction on photographic film	reaction in the presence of **sunlight** or UV light	greatly increases the rate of reaction
using a catalyst	slow reactions can be speeded up by adding a suitable catalyst	reduces amount of **energy** required for the reaction to take place: the catalyst is present in the same **mass** at the end of the reaction	**increases** the rate of reaction

Table A7.01

Exercise C7.04 The influence of surface area on the rate of reaction

a calcium carbonate + hydrochloric acid $\rightarrow$ calcium chloride + carbon dioxide + water

b Carbon dioxide is a gas and it escapes from the flask through the cotton wool.

c see Table A7.02

Time / s	0	30	60	90	120	150	180	210	240	270	300	330	360	390
Mass of CO_2 produced (exp. 1) / g	0.00	0.21	0.46	0.65	0.76	0.81	0.91	0.92	0.96	0.98	0.98	1.00	0.99	0.99
Mass of CO_2 produced (exp. 2) / g	0.00	0.51	0.78	0.87	0.91	0.94	0.96	0.98	0.99	0.99	0.99	1.00	0.99	1.00

Table A7.02

143

d

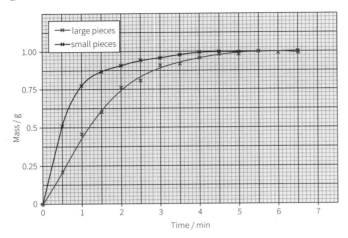

b

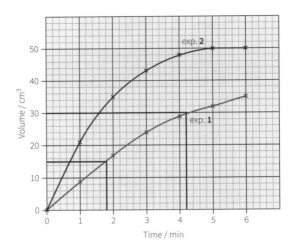

e The smaller pieces of marble (more powdered) gave the faster rate of reaction because they have a greater surface area in contact with the acid.

f The same volume of gas is produced in both cases because all the conditions are the same in both cases – the same mass of marble chips and the same volume and concentration of acid are used each time.

Exercise C7.05 Finding the rate of a reaction producing a gas

a see Table A7.03

Time / min		1	2	3	4	5	6
Volume of oxygen collected in experiment 1 / cm³		9	17	24	29	32	35
Volume of oxygen collected in experiment 2 / cm³		21	35	43	48	50	50

Table A7.03

c Experiment **2** was the first to reach completion as no more gas was produced after 5 minutes.

d see Table A7.04

Time taken to produce 30 cm³ / min	4.2
Time taken to produce 15 cm³ / min	1.8
Time taken to double the volume from 15 cm³ to 30 cm³ / min	2.4

Table A7.04

e Experiment **1**: 20 cm³ are produced in 2.5 min

rate of reaction = 20/2.5 = 8 cm³/min

Experiment **2**: 40 cm³ are produced in 2.5 min

rate of reaction = 40/2.5 = 16 cm³/min

f Copper would appear to be the better catalyst as it produces the higher rate of reaction.

g The mass of copper at the end of the experiment should be the same as that at the start. A catalyst is not used up by the reaction it catalyses.

h The catalyst itself could be ground up (powdered) more finely / the temperature could be raised.

Exercise C7.06 Runaway reactions

a see Table A7.05

Volume of water added / cm³	Concentration of acid / mol/dm³	Starting temperature / °C	Final temperature / °C	Temperature change / °C	Volume of gas collected in 30 s /cm³
0	1.00	21	53	32	42
5	*0.67*	21	44	*23*	27
10	*0.50*	21	38	*17*	21
15	*0.40*	21	34	*13*	17
20	*0.33*	21	30	*9*	13
30	*0.25*	21	27	*6*	10
40	0.20	21	25	4	7

Table A7.05

b

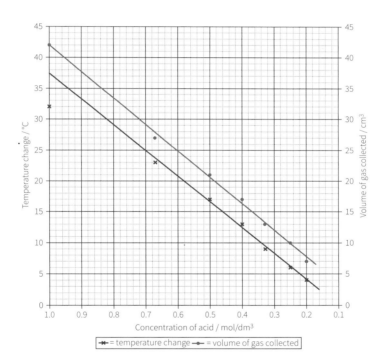

c i dilution – the solution is becoming more dilute

ii the dampening effect of adding more water – the rate of reaction is reduced by the presence of water

d because the same quantity of both acid and magnesium are used each time

e because the same amount of energy has to heat a greater volume of liquid

f The volume of gas in the first 30 s decreases showing that the rate of reaction decreases. (The total volume of gas produced should eventually be the same.)

g Use of a large volume/low concentration would keep temperature under control / use of a high concentration/low volume would result in rapid production – compromise to get the highest rate safely and monitor the temperature carefully.

145

Chapter C8 Patterns and properties of metals

Exercise C8.01 Group I: The alkali metals

a Caesium is a grey solid which conducts electricity.

b There is one electron in the outer shell of a caesium atom.

c see Table A8.01

d caesium + water $\longrightarrow$ caesium hydroxide + hydrogen

Exercise C8.02 The reactivity series of metals

a magnesium + steam (water) $\longrightarrow$ magnesium oxide + hydrogen

b copper or silver (or another metal low in the series)

c iron, or zinc, or magnesium (not calcium or sodium, etc., because these are too reactive to be safe)

d see Table A8.02

e zinc > iron > copper > silver

f copper and palladium

g barium and lanthanum

h barium or lanthanum

Group I metal	Density / g/cm³	Radius of metal atom / nm	Boiling point / °C	Reactivity with water
sodium	0.97	0.191	883	floats and fizzes quickly on the surface, disappears gradually and does not burst into flame
potassium	0.86	0.235	760	*reacts instantly, fizzes and bursts into flame, may spit violently*
rubidium	1.53	0.250	686	reacts instantaneously fizzes and bursts into flame then spits violently and may explode
caesium	1.88	*0.255–0.265 (actual value 0.260)*	*620–650 (actual value 671)*	*reacts instantly and explosively*

Table A8.01

		zinc — iron(II) sulphate solution	zinc — copper(II) sulfate solution	iron — copper(II) sulfate solution	silver — copper(II) sulfate solution	copper — silver nitrate solution
At start	**colour of metal**	grey	*grey*	silver-coloured	silver-coloured	*brown*
	colour of solution	pale green	*blue*	blue	blue	colourless
At finish	**colour of metal**	coated with metallic crystals	*coated with brown solid*	coated with brown solid	silver-coloured	coated with silver-coloured crystals
	colour of solution	colourless	*colourless*	pale green	blue	*blue*

Table A8.02

Exercise C8.03 Energy from displacement reactions

a

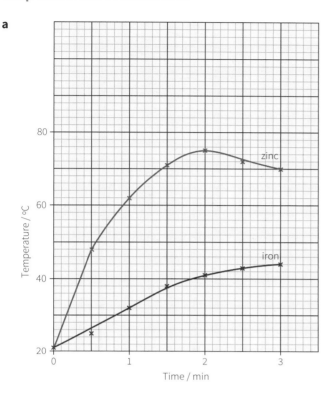

b iron + copper sulfate $\longrightarrow$ iron sulfate + copper

$Zn + CuSO_4 \longrightarrow ZnSO_4 + Cu$

c zinc

d Zinc gave the higher temperature rise because it is the more reactive metal.

e This experiment would seem to be a 'fair test' although one difficulty would be whether the two metals were powdered to the same extent. Note that, although 5 g is not an equal number of moles of the two metals, it is an excess in both cases.

Exercise C8.04 Metals and alloys

a because it is quite a good conductor and is light / it has low density

b because aluminium is not very strong and the iron/steel core gives it more strength

c because copper is a better conductor and weight is not important

d because it is light and strong – it is also expensive so can only be used for specialist purposes

e It has a lower melting point and so it is easier to melt. It is also stronger and so the joints will be stronger.

f The pins of plugs have to be strong so Cu60 : Zn40 is used.

Brass instruments have to be shaped into tubes so a softer alloy is needed. Cu70 : Zn30 is therefore used.

Chapter C9 Industrial inorganic chemistry

Exercise C9.01 Metal alloys and their uses

See Table A9.01

Alloy	Composition	Use	Useful property
mild steel	iron: >99.75% carbon: <0.25%	*car bodies*	*can be beaten into shape (malleable)*
stainless steel	iron: 74% *chromium:* 18% nickel: 8%	*cutlery*, surgical instruments, chemical vessels for industry	*corrosion resistant (does not rust easily)*
brass	copper: 70% *zinc:* 30%	*musical* instruments, ornaments	'gold' colour, harder than copper
bronze	copper: 95% *tin:* 5%	statues, church bells	hard, does not **corrode**
aerospace aluminium	aluminium: 90.25% zinc: 6% magnesium: 2.5% copper: 1.25%	aircraft construction	*light (low density) but strong*
solder	tin: 60% lead: 40%	*joining wires in electrical circuitry*	low melting point
tungsten steel	iron: 95% tungsten: 5%	cutting edges of drill bits	*very hard*

Table A9.01

Exercise C9.02 Extracting aluminium by electrolysis

a decomposition

b The electrolyte must be molten so that the ions present are able to move to the electrodes.

c The cryolite lowers the melting point of the electrolyte.

d B

e at the anode: oxygen

at the cathode: aluminium

f They have to be renewed periodically because they are made of graphite and they slowly burn away – at the high temperature of the electrolysis cell, they combine with the oxygen produced to give CO_2.

g $Al^{3+} + 3e^- \longrightarrow Al$

h making alloys for aircraft / food containers / window frames

Exercise C9.03 The importance of nitrogen

a It is a reduction reaction because electrons are gained.

b $2NO_3^- + 12H^+ + 10e^- \longrightarrow N_2 + 6H_2O$

Do not forget that the charges on each side of the equation must be the same; this helps you work out the number of electrons involved.

c fractional distillation

d steam reforming of methane

$CH_4 + H_2O \longrightarrow CO + 3H_2$

high temperature (>700 °C) with a nickel catalyst

e 450 °C, 200 atm pressure and a powdered iron catalyst

f

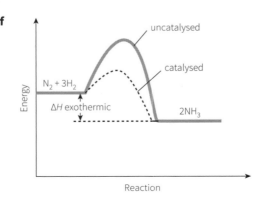

g

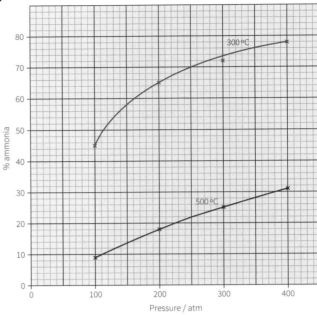

h 70% ammonia

i 46% ammonia (possible range is 42–50%)

j The disadvantage of using a low temperature would be that the ammonia would be produced at a slower rate. This slower rate could make the process uneconomic at the lower temperature.

k Using a high pressure:

- favours the production of ammonia / moves the equilibrium position to the right (because there is a smaller volume of gas on the products side of the equation)

- increases the rate of production of ammonia (because the reacting molecules are closer together and collide more often).

l ammonium nitrate, NH_4NO_3

relative formula mass = 80

% N = (28/80) × 100 = **35.0%**

ammonium hydrogenphosphate, $(NH_4)_2 HPO_4$

relative formula mass = 132

% N = (28/132) × 100 = **21.2%**

Ammonium nitrate contains the higher percentage of nitrogen.

m eutrophication; the build-up of algae in the water

Exercise C9.04 Making sulfuric acid industrially

a $2ZnS + 3O_2 \longrightarrow 2ZnO + 2SO_2$

b The products side of the equation (the right-hand side) has fewer moles of gas (occupies a smaller volume) – so a higher pressure will favour this side of the equation. As pressure increases, the equilibrium mixture contains more sulfur trioxide.

c The yield is good enough and reaction vessels that withstand high pressures are expensive to build.

d The reaction in the converter is exothermic, which would raise the temperature. So the gases are cooled down between catalyst beds.

Exercise C9.05 Concrete chemistry

a thermal decomposition

b $CaO + H_2O \longrightarrow Ca(OH)_2$

c The pH steadily increases from the surface of the beam (pH 7), through regions of pH 9, to pH 13 in the centre of the beam. This is because the alkaline calcium hydroxide at the surface is neutralised by the CO_2 in the air. Some carbon dioxide moves into the cracks to lower the pH a little there, but it cannot reach to the centre of the beam.

d Limestone is used in the blast furnace in the manufacture of iron and in the manufacture of glass.

Exercise C9.06 The chlor–alkali industry

a i Brine is a concentrated solution of sodium chloride.

ii *chlorine* (top of left-hand box); *sodium hydroxide (solution)* (top half of right-hand box); *hydrogen* (bottom half of right-hand box)

b i *sodium hydroxide* + *chlorine*
$\longrightarrow$ sodium chlorate(I) + sodium chloride + water

ii to kill bacteria / disinfect

iii $NaClO_3$

iv hydrogen + chlorine $\longrightarrow$ hydrogen chloride
$H_2 + Cl_2 \longrightarrow 2HCl$

c i The membrane keeps the products separate from each other as they can react together. Chlorine, produced at the anode, can react with the sodium hydroxide being produced in the cathode compartment.

ii because it is unreactive

iii at the anode: $2Cl^-(aq) \longrightarrow Cl_2(g) + 2e^-$
at the cathode: $2H^+(aq) + 2e^- \longrightarrow H_2(aq)$

d i an addition reaction

ii

```
   Cl  Cl
   |   |
H− C − C −H
   |   |
   H   H
```

Chapter C10 Organic chemistry

Exercise C10.01 Families of hydrocarbons

a The chief source of organic compounds is the naturally occurring mixture of hydrocarbons known as *petroleum*. Hydrocarbons are compounds that contain carbon and *hydrogen* only. There are many hydrocarbons because of the ability of carbon atoms to join together to form long *chains*. There is a series of hydrocarbons with just single covalent bonds between the carbon atoms in the molecule. These are saturated hydrocarbons, and they are called *alkanes*. The simplest of these saturated hydrocarbons has the formula CH_4 and is called *methane*. Unsaturated hydrocarbons can also occur. These molecules contain at least one carbon–carbon *double* bond. These compounds belong to the *alkenes*, a second series of hydrocarbons. The simplest of this 'family' of unsaturated hydrocarbons has the formula C_2H_4, and is known as *ethene*.

The test for an unsaturated hydrocarbon is to add the sample to *bromine* water. It changes colour from orange / brown to *colourless* if the hydrocarbon is unsaturated.

b see Table A10.01

Name	Formula	Boiling point / °C
ethene	C_2H_4	−102
propene	C_3H_6	−48
butene	C_4H_8	−7
pentene	C_5H_{10}	30
hexene	C_6H_{12}	60 (58–62)

Table A10.01

c relative molecular mass = 168; general formula C_nH_{2n} formula $C_{12}H_{24}$

149

Exercise C10.02 Unsaturated hydrocarbons (the alkenes)

a

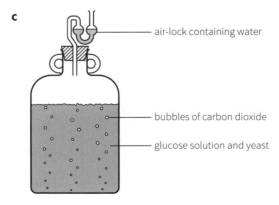

b $C_{10}H_{16}$

c The colour changes from orange/brown to colourless (not 'clear').

d A thermometer

    B (water-cooled) condenser / Liebig condenser

    C measuring cylinder

e burning in an insufficient (limited) supply of air (or oxygen)

f Carbon monoxide is toxic because it interferes with the transport of oxygen in the body (by the blood).

g

methane   ethane

× carbon electrons
• hydrogen electrons

Exercise C10.03 The alcohols as fuels

a $C_nH_{2n+1}OH$

b $C_2H_4 + H_2O \rightarrow C_2H_5OH$

conditions: 300 °C, 60 atm with phosphoric acid as catalyst

c

air-lock containing water

bubbles of carbon dioxide

glucose solution and yeast

d Ethanol is toxic to the yeast and as more is produced it eventually kills the yeast.

e Ethanol is a product of anaerobic respiration – in the presence of oxygen a different reaction takes place / in the presence of oxygen the ethanol may be oxidised.

f carbon dioxide and water

g The raw material, ethene, is obtained from cracking petroleum fractions – a non-renewable resource.

Glucose can be obtained from sugar cane (or sugar beet) and so is a renewable resource.

h

$$\begin{array}{c} H\;\;H \\ |\;\;\; | \\ H-C-C-O-H \\ |\;\;\; | \\ H\;\;H \end{array}$$

i $C_2H_5OH + 3O_2 \rightarrow \textbf{2}CO_2 + \textbf{3}H_2O$

j $x = \dfrac{13.8}{2.3} \times 2.7 = 16.2$ g of water

k

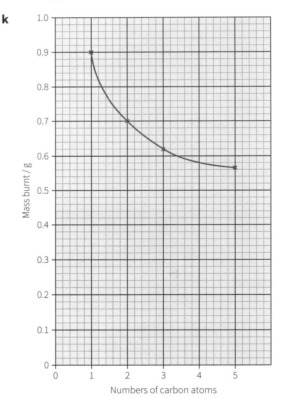

l 0.58 g

m The same value was chosen so that an easy comparison could be made between the different alcohols – to make the experiments with the different alcohols easily/directly comparable.

Exercise C10.04 Hydrocarbons and their reactions

a see Table A10.02

Name of hydrocarbon	ethane	ethene
Molecular formula of hydrocarbon	C_2H_6	C_2H_4
Relative molecular mass of hydrocarbon	*30*	*28*
Structural formula of hydrocarbon	H H ⎮ ⎮ H–C–C–H ⎮ ⎮ H H	H H ⎮ ⎮ C = C ⎮ ⎮ H H
Colour of bromine water after being shaken with the hydrocarbon	*orange/ brown*	colourless

Table A10.02

b i propane + oxygen → carbon dioxide + water

   ii $C_3H_8 + 5O_2 \rightarrow 3CO_2 + 4H_2O$

   iii 4 moles of water

c i propene + hydrogen → propane

   ii $C_4H_8 + H_2O \rightarrow C_4H_9OH$

d i The heats of combustion for propane and butane (in kj/mol) favour butane but, when calculated for a given mass of gas (kj/g), the two are very similar.

   ii The LPG mixture used in winter has a greater proportion of propane because its boiling point is lower and therefore it vaporises better at lower temperatures.

Chapter C11 Petrochemicals and polymers

Exercise C11.01 Essential processes of the petrochemical industry

a see Table 11.01

Fraction	Name	Major use
A	*refinery gas*	*as a fuel*
B	*gasoline (petrol)*	*fuel for cars*
C	*naphtha*	*for making chemicals*
D	*kerosene (paraffin)*	*aircraft fuel / heating oil*
E	*bitumen*	*tar for road surfaces*

Table A11.01

b the different boiling points of the fractions

c 'Cracking' is the breakdown of long-chain hydrocarbons (alkanes) into shorter alkanes, usually with the production of an alkene as another product.

d The demand for particular fractions does not match the proportions of the different fractions in the starting petroleum – there is less demand for the longer-chain fractions so these are cracked to give the shorter molecules for which there is a greater demand.

e i $C_{15}H_{32} \rightarrow C_{12}H_{26} + C_3H_6$

   ii
   H H H
   ⎮ ⎮ ⎮
   H–C–C = C
   ⎮   ⎮
   H   H

Exercise C11.02 Addition polymerisation

a Poly(ethene) is a *polymer* formed by the *addition* of *ethene* molecules. In this reaction, the starting molecules can be described as *monomers*; the process is known *as polymerisation*.

b
H H H H H H
⎮ ⎮ ⎮ ⎮ ⎮ ⎮
–C–C–C–C–C–C– (this shows three repeat units)
⎮ ⎮ ⎮ ⎮ ⎮ ⎮
H H H H H H

c
H   Cl
 \   /
  C = C
 /   \
H   H

d Any objects made from this polymer will create a litter problem because it will not degrade away / it will fill up landfill sites without decaying away.

e calcium chloride, carbon dioxide and water

Exercise C11.03 The analysis of condensation polymers

a i a condensation polymer (a polyamide)

   ii
   H   H   H   H
   ⎮   ⎮   ⎮   ⎮
   –N–▢–N–C–▨–C–N–▢–N–
                   ‖   ‖
                   O   O

   iii nylon

b HCl would be released.

Exercise C11.04 Meeting fuel demand

a

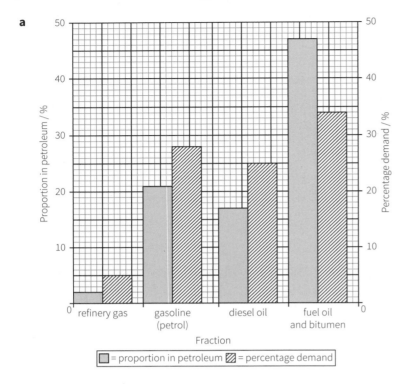

= proportion in petroleum = percentage demand

b i fuel oil and bitumen, gasoline (petrol), diesel oil

ii refinery gas / the molecules in this fraction are small (1–5 carbon atoms)

iii 53% (the gasoline (petrol) and diesel fractions)

iv (catalytic) cracking

c i This is the positive test for an alkene (unsaturation).

ii an addition reaction

iii

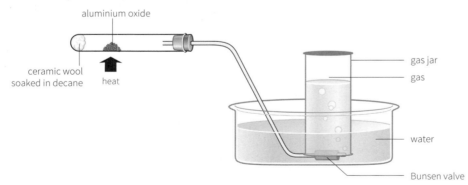

iv The aluminium oxide is a catalyst.

v see diagram in **iii**

vi to prevent 'sucking back' – this is dangerous because cold water would be drawn back into the hot apparatus

vii $C_{10}H_{22} \rightarrow C_8H_{18} + \boldsymbol{C_2H_4}$
 decane octane *ethene*

Chapter C12 Chemical analysis and investigation

Exercise C12.01 Chemical analysis

a i see Table A12.01

Test		Observation	Conclusion
1 Solid **A** was dissolved in water and the solution divided into three parts for tests **2**, **3** and **4**.		*The white solid dissolved to give a colourless solution.*	A does not contain a transition metal.
2 i To the first part, aqueous sodium hydroxide was added until a change was seen.		*A white precipitate was formed.*	A may contain Zn^{2+} ions or Al^{3+} ions.
ii Excess aqueous sodium hydroxide was added to the mixture from **i**.		*The precipitate dissolved.*	
3 i To the second part aqueous ammonia was added until a change was seen.		*A white precipitate was formed.*	The presence of Zn^{2+} ions is confirmed in **A**.
ii An excess of aqueous ammonia was added to the mixture from **i**.		*The precipitate dissolved in excess alkali.*	
4 *To the third part, a few drops of dilute nitric acid were added, followed by silver nitrate solution.*		*A yellow precipitate was formed.*	A contains I⁻ ions.

Table A12.01

ii zinc iodide, ZnI_2

b i see Table A12.02

Test	Observations
1 A sample of the solid mixture was dissolved in distilled water. The solution was acidified with dilute $HNO_3(aq)$ and a solution of $Ba(NO_3)$ added.	A white precipitate was formed.
2 A sample of the solid was placed in a test tube. NaOH(aq) was added and the mixture warmed. A piece of moist red litmus paper was held at the mouth of the tube.	The solid dissolved and pungent fumes were given off. The litmus paper turned *blue*, indicating the presence of *ammonium* ions.
3 A sample of the solid was dissolved in distilled water to give a *colourless* solution. NaOH(aq) was added dropwise until in excess.	A *white* precipitate was formed which was *soluble* in excess alkali.
4 A further sample of the solid was dissolved in distilled water. Concentrated ammonia solution ($NH_3(aq)$) was added dropwise until in excess.	A *white* precipitate was formed. On addition of excess alkali, the precipitate was *soluble*.

Table A12.02

ii ammonium sulfate $(NH_4)_2SO_4$ and zinc sulfate, $(ZnSO_4)$

iii The precipitate in both tests is zinc hydroxide, $(Zn(OH)_2)$

c i Observations for tests on filtrate:

1 The filtrate is a colourless solution.

2 A white precipitate is formed – the precipitate re-dissolves on adding excess sodium hydroxide to give a colourless solution.

3 A white precipitate is formed – this precipitate does not re-dissolve in excess ammonia – the solution is colourless.

4 No precipitate is formed on acidification and addition of silver nitrate.

5 A white precipitate is formed when barium nitrate is added.

ii The gas is carbon dioxide.

iii Solid **Q** is a carbonate because carbon dioxide was produced with acid.

Solid **Q** is a calcium or magnesium compound because there is a white precipitate formed with NaOH(aq) which does not dissolve in excess alkali.

Solid **Q** is calcium or magnesium carbonate.

Exercise C12.02 Chemical testing and evaluation

a Plan should cover the following ideas: crush samples and take equal masses of each / add acid until no further reaction takes place / filter the resulting solution / dry the residue and weigh it in each case / compare masses of impurities.

b i K^+; Mg^{2+}; NO_3^-; HCO_3^-

ii flame test: yellow colour produced

iii pH paper or pH meter

iv Measure a known quantity of the water into a pre-weighed container / evaporate (boil) to dryness avoiding any of the liquid spitting out / cool and re-weigh / subtract the mass of container and compare with the stated mass.

c i Add sodium hydroxide until in excess / the white precipitate re-dissolves to form a colourless solution.

ii Add each metal separately to an equal volume of acid / **then**:

either time the reaction / measure the gas quantity given off and compare the time until completion / volume of gas given off in fixed time.

or measure the temperature of the acid before addition / measure again at end / compare the temperature rise in each case.

d Take equal lengths/masses of magnesium ribbon / equal quantities / volumes of acid / use the same temperature for each test / need a method of changing concentration of the acid using suitable dilution (keeping the total volume the same) / time the reaction to completion and compare times or measure the gas produced in a fixed time and compare the volumes produced / make a quantitative comparison or graph of the results.

Exercise C12.03 Experimental design

a The aim of this experiment is to investigate the effect of an increase in temperature on the rate of a chemical reaction. In this experiment, the faster the rate of reaction, the quicker the 'cross' will disappear.

For the results of the experiment at different temperatures to be compared fairly, the only condition that should change is the temperature. The following factors need to be kept constant:

- the concentrations of the solutions used
- the volumes of solutions used
- the dimensions of the conical flasks in which the reactions are carried out – the depth of solution that the experimenter looks through must be the same all the time.

The solutions must be stable at the temperature being studied – so they should stand in the thermostatically controlled water bath for a suitable period to adjust to temperature.

Safety goggles should be worn because acid is being used. Ideally the experiment should be carried out in a fume cupboard or well-ventilated room as sulfur dioxide gas is produced, which is an irritant.

The instructions should include an outline of the procedure:

- the mixing of appropriate volumes of solutions – measured using a clean measuring cylinder – at the right temperature
- when to consistently start timing – this should be after adding the second solution
- to mix the solutions thoroughly by swirling the flask
- to take the time at the immediate disappearance of the marked 'cross' and record it accurately.

b i   see Table A12.03

Experiment	Thermometer diagram	Initial temperature / °C	Thermometer diagram	Final temperature / °C	Average temperature / °C	Time for printed text to disappear / s
1		24		24	24	130
2		33		31	32	79
3		40		38	39	55
4		51		47	49	33
5		60		54	57	26

Table A12.03

ii

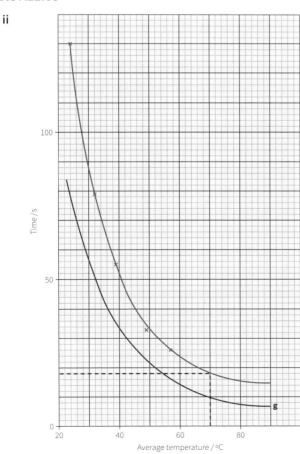

c Experiment **5**

d This was the experiment carried out at the highest temperature. Increasing the temperature increases the rate of a reaction because the particles are moving faster and therefore collide more frequently. They also have more energy when they collide and so are more likely to react.

e These conditions are necessary to make sure that the experiments can be fairly compared. If any of these were different between experiments then the observer would not be looking through the same depth of liquid to see when the cross disappeared.

f 16–20 s (a sensible range of time is allowed, as different people will draw a slightly different line between the points).

g The line will run beneath the curve for the original experiment as the reaction will be faster using a higher concentration of sodium thiosulfate (see dark gray curve on graph).

h Temperatures between 0 and 5 °C can be achieved using an iced-water bath or using solutions that have been cooled sufficiently in a refrigerator.

i More accurate control of the temperature can be achieved by carrying out the experiments in a thermostatically controlled water bath.